Series of Basic Information of Tibet of China

Tibetan Stories

Zhang Xiaoming

D1287320

CHINA INTERCONTINENTAL PRESS

图书在版编目(CIP)数据

西藏的故事／张晓明著. —北京: 五洲传播出版社,
2004.7

(中国西藏基本情况)

ISBN 7-80113-914-3

Ⅰ. 西… Ⅱ. 张… Ⅲ. 西藏—概况—英文

Ⅳ.K927.5

中国版本图书馆 CIP 数据核字 (2004) 第 087813 号

《中国西藏基本情况丛书》

主　　编: 郭长建　　宋坚之

副主编: 雷　珈

责任编辑: 荆孝敏

摄　　影: 土　登　　车　刚　　杜泽泉　　陈宗烈
　　　　　张　鹰　　赵远志　　唐召明　等

版式设计: 杨　津

制版印刷: 深圳麟德电脑设计制作有限公司

中国西藏基本情况丛书—西藏的故事

(英文版)

翻　　译: 王国振　　李金慧

五洲传播出版社

地址: 中国北京北三环中路 31 号　邮编: 100088

电话: 82000055　网址: www.cicc.org.cn

开本: 140 × 210mm　1/32　印张: 4.2

2004 年 12 月第一版　印数: 1-11500

ISBN 7-80113-914-3/K·261

定价: 38.00 元

CONTENTS

Tibetan Buddhism and Temporal and Religious Administration 49

Democratic Reform and Self-Government in Tibet 69

Reform Program Enjoys Popularity 87

Between Tradition and Modernization 109

Colorful sutra streamers can be seen everywhere in Tibet.

Here Is a Real Tibet

Many in the world are talking about Tibet, their discussions concentrated mainly on human rights, culture, Tibetan Buddhism, landscape and folklore. But very few have been to Tibet. And, although they hold their own firm views, the fact is that they lack real understanding of the region.

In this book is a picture of Tibet-- which might be quite different from that within the current understanding of our readers. However, it is a real Tibet. I am able to paint the real picture because I worked there for about 10 years. Although I am working in Beijing, my job requires me to go back there at least once a year, and I want to tell you what I have seen.

The Potala Palace in the center of Lhasa.

Qinghai-Tibet Plateau and Tibetan Race

Flying from Chengdu, capital of Sichuan Province, to Lhasa is really entertaining. Peeping through the tiny plane windows one sees magnificent Qinghai-Tibet Plateau cut by rivers that zigzag through endlessly undulating mountain ranges.

Siba Butchers Cows

I used the 1,300-km air route, created in the 1950s, many times. And whenever I was in the plane, my mind went back to lectures given by Jambien Gyamco (Tibetan), a noted Tibetologist who was my tutor. Once, he told us an ancient song known to all Tibetans: Siba Butchers Cows.

"Where is the calf head,
Cut off by Siba?
I don't know and have to ask the singer.
Where is the calf tail,
Cut off by Siba?
I don't know and have to ask the singer.
Where is the calf hide,
Skinned by Siba?

I don't know and have to ask the singer.

"When Siba butchers the calf,

He cuts off the head and leaves it at a higher place.

Hence high peaks.

When Siba butchers the calf,

He cuts off the tail and leaves it at a place shadowed by mountains.

Hence forests.

When Siba butchers the calf,

He skins the hide to cover the ground.

Hence smooth terrain."

Actually, this is a story which tells how the ancestors of the Tibetan race created heaven and earth. It is also a Tibetan explanation as to how the Qinghai-Tibet Plateau was created. What I quote here is a segment of the song. Other parts all are related to the creation of the plateau.

Tibetans are so great that ancient Tibetan scholars have left behind many stories, which, even to modern eyes, are very scientific. Here is one:

"Eons ago, the world was pitch dark and void of everything. A gentle wind came out of emptiness and gained momentum gradually. Clouds gathered, and it rained cats and dogs for many years. After the rain, there came the sea....

"Wind blew through the sea surface, touching off waves. Bubbles rose to cover the sea. And land emerged...."

What Geophysicists Say

Zheng Zhong, a noted geophysicist explains the rise of the Qinghai-Tibet Plateau in this way: The plateau, the highest part of the world, was elevated as a result of the rise of the ancient sea, later known as Tethys.

A scientist in the West described the ancient ocean in this way: "A giant ocean in ancient times connected the European and Asian continents....We call the ocean Tethys." Tethys is a female deity in charge of oceans in Greek mythology.

Prof. Pan Yusheng, a Chinese geologist and specialist in earth structure, describes the Qinghai-Tibet Plateau like this: In ancient times, the Qinghai-Tibet Plateau was the site of an ocean on three separate

Mount Qomolangma, 8848.13 meters, is the highest peak of the world. It is part of the Himalaya Mountains situated in the border area of China's Tingri County, Tibet Autonomous Region and Nepal.

4

occasions. Called Ex-Tethys, the ocean lay where the Western Kunlun-Qilianshan Mountains are now located. The ocean, created as a result of the splitting of land, existed 900-400 million years ago, a period when life was in its infancy and the waves were all that created noise in the deadly quiet environment.

With the elapse of time, Tethys receded to make way for the separated north and south continental plates to meet. At the same time, the Ancient Tethys rose in an area where the Qinghai-Tibet Plateau is located today. During the period of the Ancient Tethys, some 350-200 million years ago, life emerged on earth in the shape of fish and reptiles, and plants proliferated through the spread of seeds.

After Ancient Tethys came New Tethys, born on the southern rim of the European and Asian continental plates. This happened some 180 million years ago, a period when dinosaurs roamed and the present Indian Ocean was located in the far south of the Southern Hemisphere. Its southernmost tip was at 40 degrees South Latitude 71 million years ago. This segment of the continent moved northward at an annual rate of 10 cm. When it collided with the European and Asian continental plates some 40 million years ago, the New Tethys disappeared. What was left is the present Yarlung Zangbo River housed in the narrow rim sandwiched between two continental plates that used to be far apart. At this point of time, an area with an elevation of some 1,000 meters emerged. Enjoying a humid

Tibetan boy in a welcoming ceremony.

and hot climate, it was a sweep of forests and grass. However, it kept rising in the ensuing 3 million years. Finally, the Qinghai-Tibet Plateau, 4,700 meters above sea level, was born.

This rose irregularly. It had grown 1,000 meters 2 million years ago, and another 1,000 meters was added in the ensuing 1 million years. In the 100,000 years since the Pleistocene Era, it went up by 1,500 meters. In the past 10,000 years, however, annual growth has been 7 cm, for a total of 700 meters.

The Plateau Itself

The Qinghai-Tibet Plateau is formed by several mountain ranges, including the Himalayas, Kangdese, Nyainqentanglha, Tanggula, Kunlun-Kalakunlun, and Qilianshan. All of these mountain ranges spread from east to west, except for the Hengduan Mountains in the eastern part of the Plateau. Snaking through these mountains are three major rivers, Jinshajiang, Lancangjiang and Nujiang. The ravines hold dense primitive forests.

The northern rim is inlaid with the Qinghai Lake. West of it is Golmud City, starting point of the Qinghai-Tibet Railway now being constructed. Southwest of Golmud lies Kunlun Mountain, across which is a vast sweep of plateau land-source of the Tongtian River, or the upper reaches of the Yangtze River. The Tongtian River faces the Nujiang River across the Tanggula Mountain, which is the highest point the Qinghai-Tibet Railway will have to cross. In the southwestern part of Tanggula Mountain is a group of 6,000-meter peaks, including the Geladandong, where the Yangtze River originates.

Further northwest is the hinterland of the Changtang Plateau. Tucked away at an elevation of 4,500 meters, it covers some 600,000 square km. Mountains here rise gently. This part of the world is home to half of China's lakes. Most of them are spread in livestock breeding area or no-man's land. They include the Nam Co and Serling Co. The southern part of Changtang is home to the Nagqu River, source of the Nujiang River and its tributaries. North Tibet is the major livestock breeding area in Tibet; a world of white sheep and black yaks.

After Nyainqentanglha in the south is the Lhasa-South Tibet Valley. The Yarlung Zangbo River, like a snow-white *hada* scarf, snakes downward between the Kangdese and the Himalayas. It flows 2,070 km within China. When it makes a U-turn at Medog, it flows from Bashika into India to become the Brahmaputra

Nagqu Pastureland in north Tibet.

Scenery of Nyingchi.

River, finally emptying into the Bay of Bengal via Bangladesh.

The Himalayas in the west measure 2,400 km long and 300 km wide, with an average elevation of 6,200 meters. In its middle part are six peaks each of 8,000 meters high, including the Qomolangma, which is 8,848.13 meters high. Formed with limestone, the black-colored peak is wrapped in snow that makes it glisten

Horse-racing among farmers and herdsmen, a program at the annual Yarlung Culture and Art Festival in Shannan Prefecture.

blindly under the sun.

Further west is Ngari, home to the ancient kingdom of Guge. The Ngari Plateau extends 300,000 km and possesses astonishing beauty.

Story About the Name of Tubo

On the young plateau the Tubo race lived and multiplied. With a recorded history of 1,300 years, they boasted a fine cultural tradition. With regard to the reason why they were called "Bo", very few people have striven to find out.

According to Mr. Qabai Cedain Puncog (*General*

Bird Island on Bangong Co in west Tibet.

History of Tibet: Gems), the Tubo people lived on hunting in the beginning and gradually learned to raise domestic animals. For this purpose, they had to roam around in pursuit of water and grass. Exposed to natural calamities and attacks by gangs and wild animals, they tended to live in places where others could hear their yell for help. And they called their yelling "Boba." Gradually, "Bo" became the name of these places.

There is another story about the title of Tubo: Tibetan terrain is high in the north and low in the southeast. Historically, the Tibetans divided the plateau into three parts based on the type of business they carried out: animal husbandry in high places, farming in low valleys, where they engaged in forestry, and the "Bo" area, where they carried out mainly farming.

When the Siboye clan declared a Tsampo (king) of the area, they called themselves "Tubo Tsampo". The area under "Tubo Tsampo" expanded in the ensuing periods to cover U-Tsang. When Songtsan Gambo brought under his control the small tribes and he ascended to the throne, he called the area "Tubo".

Dainzhub Ongboin, a young Tibetologist, says in his *Formation of the Tibetan Race*, that Tibetan civilization originated from two sources: Zhangzhung and the Yarlung River Valley. The Zhangzhung Civilization refers to a period in which the Bon religion spread through the Qinghai-Tibet Plateau, with the Tibetan race finally having access to a unified language and folklore. The Yarlung River Valley Civilization witnessed the period in which the Siboye clan conquered other tribes in the Qinghai-Tibet Plateau to form the State of Siboye. As previously mentioned, Siboye kings called area they ruled "Tubo".

Ancestor Monkey and Raksasi

Long, long ago, a monkey with magic powers was sent by the Goddess of Mercy to practice mediation in what it is Tibet today. The monkey made great headway in Buddhist mediation before a nearby Raksasi (female demon) approached him and said admiringly: "Let's marry!"

They married, and gave birth to six monkeys. All these small moneys lived separately in the forest. Three years later, when their parents visited them one by one, they had more than 500 children and grandchildren,

Chapai Cedain Pucog, famous historian of Tibet and member of Tibetan Academy of Social Sciences.

Members of Costume Exhibition Team from Ganze Tibetan Nationality Autonomous Prefecture, Sichuan Province, showed their colorful and gorgeous clothes and ornaments at the 3rd Kamba Art Festival held in October 2000.

who had finished all the fruit available in the forest. The father monkey returned to the Heavenly Kingdom and brought back to earth *qingke* barley, wheat, beans, buckwheat and other kinds of cereals for cultivation.

With more than enough food, all the monkeys lost their hair and tails. Gradually, they learned to speak, and finally became man.

The story sounds mysterious, but it tells of the birth and evolution of the Tibetan race. Of the 698 frescoes painted by some 400 master painters in the Potala Palace in Lhasa, two depict the birth and evolution of the Tibetans. There is also a fresco in the Sutra Hall of the Norbu Lingka (Summer Palace for the Dalai Lama), which also depicts how moneys evolve into man in Tibet. Zetang in Shannan derives its name from the motif, meaning "the place where monkeys play." Locals will show visitors a mountain cave where they say the father monkey lived, and Sala

New residential buildings of Qamdo.

Farmers of Gyangze County, Xigaze Prefecture in rear Tibet, are celebrating the Ongkor Festival.

Village 3 km from Zetang, which they say is where the first plot of *qingke* barley field. During the sowing season, the locals come to throw a handful of soil into the air to pray for help from the ancestors.

Two Ruins of the New Stone Age

No matter how the legends describe it, scholars differ about the origins of the Tibetan race. In the 1960s, archaeologists found 16 sites of the Old Stone Age, 39 sites of the Microlithic Age, and six sites of the New Stone Age in Surab of Tingri, Dorgeze of Xainzha, Zhabu of Ritog, and Hor of Burang. From the ruins in Nyingchi, they unearthed fossils of ancient man and ancient vertebrates.

The Karub Ruins in Qamdo and the Qugong Ruins in Lhasa are the largest of their kind in terms of artifacts excavated.

Legend has it that there was a rocky mountain near Karub. There is also a legend that says: Marshal Dorda of the Mongol Kharnate led his troops to Tibet and planned to send his men to Qamdo. The locals erected pillboxes in the area of Karub to resist. These pillboxes were abandoned and left unoccupied later. When the locals moved in, a village formed. The occupants call it Karub Village meaning "abandoned pillbox village."

In the beginning, the village sat on the western bank of the Lancangjiang River, with an elevation of 3,100 meters. It was calculated that the village ruins take the shape of a square with an area of 10,000 square meters. Two excavations were conducted over an area of 1,800 square meters. Artifacts found include 29 house ruins, three segments of house walls, two stone walls, four dugout stoves, 7,978 stone objects, 368 bone objects, and some 20,000 pieces of stone chips. Archaeologists concluded that these houses were thatched ones in a domed, square or rectangular shape. In the center of each house was a triangular stone stove. Unearthed bone objects, few in number, include awls,

The loess land deposited in a thousand years provided natural conditions for ancient Guge people to dig caves to live in.

Kangrinboqe Peak, at an elevation of 6,714 meters, is the highest one of the Gandise Mountains. It is a famous Buddhism Holy Land.

A Buddhism disciple throws parched highland barley flour into Mapam Yumco, a Holy Lake, while paying a homage to it and praying for peace and auspiciousness.

needles, axes and saws. All of them are finely polished, commanding good workmanship. Some bone needles measure only 24 mm with smooth holes. Pottery finds include jars, pots and bowls, painted with rich patterns. Some of them have carved or rope-etched patterns. They are in red, yellow, gray or black color. Decorative objects found include hairpins, earrings, beads and necklaces, made of stone or bone. Most of the artifacts are tools, such as stone shovels, stone axes, hoes, ploughs, spear heads, arrow heads, sickles and chopping knives, totaling 6,800 items in all.

The Karub Culture falls into the category of the New Stone Age some 4,500-5,000 years ago. It reveals exchanges between southwest and northwest. The excavated items provide valuable materials for archaeologists to conclude that the Karub people lived mainly on farming with some hunting.

The Qugong Ruins some 5 km from Lhasa was excavated in 1984 on a small scale, and again in 1990. From the dug area of 500-odd square meters, archaeologists concluded that it was composed of garbage pits and tombs. The artifacts include stone objects, pottery chips, bone objects and animal bones, which date back over 4,000 years. All signs show that here was a settlement of the Tibetan ancestors present long before the Yarlung tribe moved their capital to Lhasa.

In a nutshell, there were people who lived and multiplied in that part of the world. The Tibetan race evolved from the local natives instead of people who migrated from other parts of the world. Of course, the Tibetan race composed of people whose ancestors were Han, Chiang or Mongolian.

Story of the Son of the Heavenly Deity

There are many stories about Nyitri Tsampo. Here is one: In about the 3rd century BC, several large states emerged on the Tibet Plateau. One of them was Zhangzhung in the northwest, where the Bon religion was flourishing. Bon involves the worship of deities and fights against evil spirits. Adherents paid special attention to sacrificial rituals, and spread the Bon doctrines by telling stories. Other states included Supi in

Horse-racing fair on
northern Tibet pasture.

the central part and the Yarlung River Valley, in which
present-day Shannan is located.

Residents of the Yarlung tribe lived on hunting,
livestock breeding and farming. They learned to make
bows and arrows, knives, axes and other kinds of production tools. Comparatively developed farming
brought prosperity to the valley, but the six tribes in
the area were not unified under one leader.

A tall, strongly built young man moved down the
mountain when the tribal members were herding animals on the mountain slopes. He told them he came
from the blue sky behind him. Not clear where he did
come from, the tribal members invited 12 learned
people to examine him. The result was a decision that
he did come from heaven and he was the son of the
Heavenly Deity.

The young man was carried back to the valley,
and made the first king (Tsampo) of the Tubo Kingdom.
As he was carried there on the shoulders of the Yarlung

The bustling market
in front of Jokhang
Monastery, Lhasa.

Nam Co, the largest lake of Tibet at the foot of N y a i n q e n T a n g l h a Mountain.

tribal members, he was named Nyitri Tsampo, meaning "king sitting on the necks of his subjects."

Nyitri Tsampo was, of course, not the son of heavenly deities. He was born into a family of 11 in Bowo in eastern Tibet. He had eight elder brothers. Though good-looking, he had a tongue large enough to cover his face, and webbed fingers. People in that area thought he was the incarnation of a demon, and forced him to leave his hometown. This is why he went to the Yarlung River Valley.

To rejuvenate the Yarlung tribal association, Nyitri Tsampo worked out a policy geared toward stimulating farming and livestock breeding, and, at the same time, making the Bon religion as the state religion. Yungbo Lhakang Castle was built to prevent invasion; and that turned out to be the first castle built by the Tibetans in history. Here lies the beginning of Tibetan history.

Tibet Museum preserves a large number of cultural and historical relics.

History and Facts

Historical Records on Tubo Found in Dunhuang

Oldest materials on the Tubo include the *Dunhuang Records on Tubo History*, found in the Dunhuang Grottoes in Gansu Province, where they had been stored for some 800 years. A Taoist named Wang first found them in 1900, but, from 1905 to 1909, explorers and archeologists from Russia, Britain, France and Japan ransacked the grottoes and took away many valuable materials that are now found only in museums or archives in France and the United Kingdom.

These historical materials record the political and military affairs of the earliest tribes in Tubo, plus folklore. They date back some 1,300 years, and, although these historical facts were also recorded elsewhere, they were cloaked with religious color.

Only six parts of the *Biography of Tsampos of the Dunhuang Records on Tubo History* are still kept intact and available to Tibetologists. They include the *Biography of Zhigung Tampo, Biography of Dagbo Nyisai, Biography of*

Nari Lhuntsam, Biography of Songtsan Gambo, Biography of Tride Songtsan and Tride Zotsam, and *Biography of Trisong Detsam*.

There were 32 generations of Yarlung tsampos (kings) and nine generations of Tubo tsampos, with Songtsan Gampo being the last tsampo of the Yarlung tribe and also the first tsampo of the Tubo Kingdom. The "six parts of the *Biography of Tsampos of the Dunhuang Records on Tubo History*" relate how the Yarlung River Valley was united and developed farming, livestock breeding and culture. The people there mastered the necessary skills to make silver, bronze and iron tools, furniture and weapons, and to dig irrigation ditches. They also show how the Tubo Kingdom grew in strength through repeated military expeditions, until it became the first unified political regime in the land of snows.

Nyainqentanglha Mountains.

Exchanges Between Han and Tibetan, and Princess Wencheng

The Han and the Tubo fought more than 500 battles. A total of 15 Han princesses were married to rulers of the minority areas for political reason, including Princess Wencheng and Princess Jincheng, who were married to Tubo kings.

The story of Princess Wencheng has been told for some 1,300 years:

The Tang Dynasty (618-907) in the Central Plains was located east of the Tubo Kingdom. Before Princess Wencheng went to Tubo to marry Songtsan Gambo, Emperor Taizong had married off Princess Honghua to the Tuguhun tribe and Princess Hengyang to the Tuju tribe. Admiring the friendly ties between

Statues of Songtsan Gambo and Princess Wencheng worshipped in the Jokhang Monastery of Lhasa.

the Tang and the two ethnic groups, Songtsan Gambo sent his minister to propose a similar marriage. When neglected, Songtsan Gambo fought Tuguhun, and invaded the Central Plains area of the Tang Dynasty. When he reached an area west of Songzhou, he sent a letter to the Tang emperor stating: "We come solely to make a marriage proposal. If the Tang refuses, we will raze the city to the ground." Learning that the Tubo troops, numbering 200,000, had invaded the Han area merely to press a marriage proposal, the Tang emperor was greatly relieved and gave consent to the marriage.

What is recorded here is a beautiful story. The fact is as follows:

In 640, Songtsan Gambo sent his minister Gar Tongtsan to Chang'an (present-day Xi'an), capital of the Tang Dynasty. The minister took with him 5,000 taels of gold and hundreds of jewels as tribute to the Tang emperor.

Also traveling to Chang'an for the same purpose were envoys from India, Persia, Cong Gesar, Bada Hor and other states. Confronted with so many suitors for Princess Wencheng, the Tang emperor engineered a contest of wisdom. Whoever emerged as the winner would win the hand of Princess Wencheng for their ruler.

During the contest, each was required to perform five difficult tasks.

The first required the ministers to identify the mother and child bond among 100 hens and 100 chicks, and the same among 100 mares and 100 colts, within three days.

While the other envoys failed, Gar Tongtsan scattered chicken feed on the ground. As the hens and chicks were eating merrily, someone imitated the cry of a hawk. The frightened chicks immediately rushed to their respective mothers, who spread their wings as shelter. So, that knotty problem was solved.

Yungbolhakang, the first palace built in Tibet during the Tubo Kingdom.

Gar Tongtsan then ordered the mares to be separated from the colts and stopped the supply of feed and water to the young for a whole day. When he put the animals together on the second day, all the starving colts rushed toward their respective mothers for milk.

The second task was for the ministers to discern the top and root ends of 100 logs. When all the others again

Nyang River in Nyingchi Prefecture.

failed, Gar Tongtsan ordered the logs to be placed in the water. As the top end is lighter than the root end, he solved the question instantly.

The ministers were then asked to make a soft silk thread pass through a pearl with a nine-bend passage within, with a sharp turn in the middle. While other ministers wasted their breath on this task, Gar Tongtsan succeeded by tying a hair from the horsetail around the waist of an ant, and put it into the mouth of the pearl passage. He blew and blew at the creature until it crawled out from inside the pearl. Then he tied the silk thread to the other end of the horsetail hair and so it was easy for him to lead the silk thread through the pearl.

The fourth task was for these ministers to slaughter 100 sheep and finish 50 kg of liquor all in one day. Moreover, they were required to eat up the mutton, rub clean the sheep hides, and clean the ground to the point that it was free from even a single spot of sheep's blood. Given the fact that livestock breeding was developed in Tubo, Gar Tongtsan and his men completed the mission before the sunset of the same day.

The fifth and the last task required the visiting envoys to spot Princess Wencheng from among 500 beauties. All shook their heads except for Gar Tongtsan, who did his best to get information about the Tang princess. The Tang emperor presided over the event in person. The result was that Gar Tongtsan found Princess Wencheng from among the 500 beauties.

Pleased by the wisdom of the Tubo minister, the Tang emperor agreed to let Princess Wencheng go to Tubo for marriage with King Songtsan Gambo. She left Chang'an for Lhasa in the spring of the 15th year of the reign of the Tang Emperor Zhenguan.

Other stories about Princess Wencheng include those about the Sun-Moon Mountain, her construction of Jokhang Monastery, and her efforts to promote the herding of sheep and weaving of cloth. Behind these stories, which have passed down the history in the form of folk songs and Tibetan opera performance, lie the brotherly ties between the Han and the Tibetan. A case in point is the Tang-Tubo Peace Pledge Tablet in front of the Jokhang Monastery.

Tubo Tsampo Songtsan Gambo once sent emissaries to Chang'an, capital city of the Tang Dynasty, asking for a marriage. In 641 AD, Princess Wencheng was married to him, starting the close relationship between the Tang Dynasty and Tubo Kingdom. The picture is *The Audience*, painted by Yan Liben of the Tang Dynasty, illustrating the historical fact that Tang Dynasty Emperor Taizong gave an audience to Tubo envoy Gar Tongtsan.

Tang-Tubo Peace Pledge Tablet

This is one of the must-worship monasteries in Lhasa, where Tibetan incense burns all year round. In front of the monastery, the Tablet has stood for some 1,000 years.

In the late 1970s, when I first saw the Tablet, it was sealed off from the public by walls. It was coated with butter and pasted with coins and paper money--a move resorted to by the Tibetans to show their respect for the past. Part of the Tablet was underground and an archaeologist told me later that it stands on a stone tortoise. Over the centuries, close to two meters of the Tablet "sank" underground as a result of the rising of the ground in Lhasa. It still stands in front of Jokhang Monastery, but has been totally protected with walls built around it.

The Yarlung Zangbo River.

The history of the Tablet dated back to 704, when the 4th Tubo King Tride Zutsan sent his officials to Chang'an for marriage with a Tang princess. Princess Jincheng entered Tubo in 710 as a result.

There are also stories about this particular segment of history. One describes how Princess Jincheng gave birth to a son. The boy was named Trisong Detsan, but was soon taken away by a concubine of the Tubo king. When the boy was one year old, the king held a banquet to celebrate the boy's birthday. Relatives of the two women were invited.

During the banquet, the king told the boy: "You don't know who is your mother though you are one year old. To have your real mother, you have to find out your maternal uncle first."

The banquet hall was gripped in a tense atmosphere, as the concubine side understood that loss of the prince would mean loss of power for them in the future. They showed the cloak the boy used to wear and brought out colorful toys he used to play to attract his attention.

Princess Jincheng looked worried, and those hailing from the Han area stretched out their arms in the hope that the boy would come over.

Holding a cup of wine in hand, the one-year-old prince said: "I am a nephew of the Han."

Princess Jincheng, hot tears rolling down her beautiful cheeks, clutched the boy to her bosom. The boy later became the 5th Tubo king.

In his memorial to the Tang emperor, Tubo King Tride Zutsan said: "I am a nephew of the deceased

In 821 AD, Tubo Kingdom sent envoys to the Tang asking for alliance. In 822 AD, Tubo and Tang met for the 8th time in Lhasa. Liu Yuanding, a Tang official in Dali and Chanbu, most revered monk of Tubo, participated in the meeting and read the oath. In 823 AD, the Tang-Tubo Alliance Monument was erected, which still stands in the square in front of the Jokhang Monastery today.

Emperor, and now I have been honored with a marriage to Princess Jincheng. This shows that we are of one family. I am therefore confident that all people in both of our lands will live in peace and happiness." Similar words appear in the inscription on the Tablet.

During that historical period, Tang and Tubo exchanged envoys for peace negotiations while sometimes locked in military confrontation. According to historical records, both sides met for peace talks on eight occasions from 706 to 822. In 815, Trisong Detsan came to the throne as the 8th Tubo king. In 821, he dispatched his monk minister, Blong Nalo, to Chang'an to appeal for a mutual pledge of peace. Both sides met in the western suburbs of Chang'an in September. A stone tablet was carved in 823. Measuring 343 cm high, 82 cm wide and 32 cm thick, it bears the inscription, in both Tibetan and Han Chinese, of the written pledge of peaceful and friendly relations from both parties. In this statement, they reiterated the historical relationship of maternal uncle and nephew, as well as their resolve to mind their own lands without harassing each other.

According to historical records, the Central Plains and the Tubo Kingdom maintained peace after the erection of the Tablet.

Tea-Horse Trade

The Tibetan areas do not produce much tea, but the Tibetans are addicted to tea drinking. A Tibetan saying goes that one will have pain if he does not drink

The Tang-Tubo Alliance Monument records the history of meetings and marriage between the two sides. The monument inscription reads in part, "The two sovereigns, uncle and nephew, having come to agreement that their territories be united as one, have signed this alliance of great peace to last for eternity! May God and humanity bear witness thereto so that it may be praised from generation to generation".

The statue of Sakyamuni (at the age of 12) is enshrined in the Main Hall of the Jokhang Monastery. It was one of the dowries of Princess Wencheng of the Tang Dynasty when she was married to Songtsan Gambo.

tea for three days; one can forego food, but cannot cope without tea to drink.

Tea began to make its way into Tibet in the 5th century, when the Tibetans did not have any tea drinking habit. Only royal families collected tea as a kind of tonic. According to *History of the Han and Tibetans*, "Han monks loved tea very much. The King of Garmi learned from them how to make tea. Mizha Gongbo learned to make tea from the king. Gradually, the Tibetans learned to make and drink tea."

In the beginning, only those with the royal families and monastery monks loved tea. When Tubo King Darma suppressed Buddhism, monks fled here and there. From them, the Tibetans learned to make and drink tea. What tea can bring to the Tibetans--quench--ing thirst, helping with digestion and staying up late at night--is what the Tibetans need. Gradually, they become addicted to it.

During the late Tang Dynasty (618-907), the Tubo managed to be on good terms with the Central Plains.

Sagya Monastery, major monastery of the Sagya sect, holds grand dancing ceremonies each winter to drive out demons. Disciples nearby crowd in to watch the dance.

People in the latter area used silks and tea to trade for Tubo horses and cows. This kind of trade was quite developed in Sichuan, Yunnan, Qinghai and other areas where there were Tibetans. The Silk Road and the Tea-Horse Trading Route were created then. Large amounts of tea were transported to the Tibetan region as a result.

However, tea or horses were traded mainly as tributary to the court in the beginning, instead of business people. In the ensuing period of the Five Dynasties, Song and Jin (907-1234), the Hexi Corridor was seized by the Tubo and other ethnic minorities. The central court set up the Tea-Horse Office in Tatiju to take in charge of barter trade. In 1372, the Ming (1368-1644) court set up the Department of Tea-Horse Trade, to take in charge of trading tea for Tubo horses. At that time, horses were used for corvee labor or as tribute. The new system was adopted to cope with the fact that many from the Tibetan areas went to the central court to hold an official position. For this purpose, they paid tribute to the emperor, who granted them tea as a gift in return. As both parties saw the benefits of this, Tubo tribute paying officials gradually evolved into business people.

The above shows that the tea-horse trade was both an economic activity, as well as a political move. It promoted political, economic and cultural exchanges between the Han and Tibetan areas. The road traversed by business people, connecting Tibet with Sichuan, Gansu and Qinghai, paved the way for construction of post routes in ancient times and the highways of today.

Sagya Monastery under renovation.

Sagya Monastery and Pagba

Sagya was a small town least known to all during the heyday of the Tubo Kingdom. In the 9th century, Buddhist activities were suppressed, and this was followed by a slave uprising, leading to the collapse of the Tubo Kingdom. In 1073, Gongqoi Gyibo, a member of the Kun clan, managed to build Gorong Monastery, predecessor of the Sagya North Monastery,

Great sutra hall of the Sagya Monastery.

on Boinbori Mountain. Thus, did Sagya enter Tibetan history. The monastery took shape during the time of Sapan Gonggar Gyaincain (1182-1251), and from it, Sagya became one of the most important Buddhist sects in Tibet. The North Monastery was refurbished as a major center just before the Yuan Dynasty. It was composed of the Buddha Hall, dormitories for the monks, and a forest of dagobas that crawled along the mountain slopes in a majestic way. In about 200 years, from the period of Gongqoi Gyibo to the period of Pagba, it was repeatedly rebuilt and expanded into a monastery with 28 Buddha halls. With the growing in strength of the Sagya Sect, the South Monastery was established.

During the period, various Buddhist sects were astonished by the fact the Yuan (Mongol) troops had defeated the Western Xia and Jin Dynasties, conquered the Central Asia, and even fought their way into Europe. From 1239 to 1240, the Yuan court sent General Dorta Nagpo to Tibet. He and Dyima took with them a letter to religious leaders from the Mongol Princess Gotan, which showed there was no way out but to accept Yuan rule.

Sapan was 63 years old. It was a hard nut to crack for him to go all the way to Liangzhou to meet Princess Gotan. Nonetheless, he reached his destination in two years, and met the Princess in the first month of the following year.

Sapan and Princess Gotan reached agreement on the terms for Tibet to be subordinated to the Yuan court, and on this basis, Sapan wrote an open letter to the monk and lay officials in Tibet, which is known in

Warrior in the dancing ceremony of the Sagya Monastery.

Jade statue of Drogon Chogyal Pagba preserved in the Potala Palace.

history as Sagya Pandit's Letter to the Tubo People.

The letter described how Sapan had enjoyed special treatment in Liangzhou and how seriously Gotan worshipped Buddhism. He urged the Tibetans to accept the situation and pledge allegiance to the Mongols. With regard to the terms, the letter said that officials and civilians in the Tibetan areas were subordinates of the Mongols, who should send people to take care of local affairs, while the leaders of the Sagya Sect would be entrusted to take in charge of religious affairs. All who were willing to accept Mongol rule should produce three kinds of certificates: one with the names of local officials; one regarding the number of people involved; and one concerning the variety and quantity of the tributes paid. Each certificate should have three

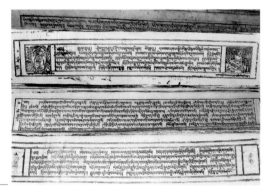

Dangyur in Dege edition (original woodcut edition).

copies, with one copy sent to Prince Gotan, one sent to Sagya and one kept by local officials. Those who accepted Mongolian rule would be protected when they came. The letter listed the variety of the tributes the Mongols desired.

The meeting between Sapan Gonggar Gyaincain and Prince Gotan (grandson of Genghis Khan) in Liangzhou made it possible for Tibet to be subordinated to the Yuan Dynasty without bloodshed. In the ensuing years, the Central Government set up 130,000-household offices for effective rule. Post stations were set up, and monk official titles were granted. Pagba (1235-1280), nephew of Sapan, was granted an official position as the Imperial Tutor. In the Central Government, the Zhongzhi Yuan was set up, headed by Pagba, which took charge of Buddhist affairs throughout China, Tibet included. With Central Government support, the Sagya regime was set up in 1275. Combining religious and government powers, it ruled Tibet in a new way.

Yongle Edition of Tripitaka

In 1994 the world was excited to learn that the Tibetan Tripitaka had been collated and published with funding from the Chinese Government. A ceremony was held in the Great Hall of the People in Beijing, and I attended the ceremony. The book has a sheep hide cover and was printed in a modern way. Actually, efforts were made more than 600 years ago to print the Tripitaka.

Back to 1410, Emperor Yongle of the Ming Dynasty had a hand-copied edition of the Tripitaka: *Dangyur* and *Gangyur* sent to Nanjing, the capital. It was the first printed edition of Tripitaka with 108 folds. Its cover bore gilded titles in Chinese and Tibetan, and the sutras inside were printed in red ink. Only a few copies were printed, and they were used as gifts to the three religious leaders of the Sagya, Gelug and Gagyu sects. One of these is kept intact in the Sera Monastery today.

When the Ming Dynasty ruled China, Tibet was under the Pagmo Zhuba regime, which featured a relatively thriving economy and culture. Copying and printing the Tripitaka was in fashion then.

The Tripitaka is a collection of Buddhist classics in

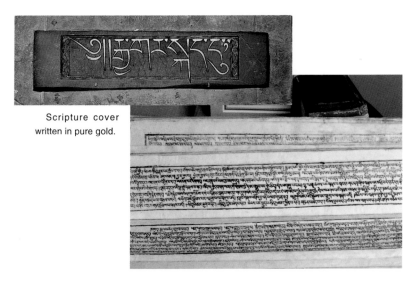

Scripture cover written in pure gold.

Dangyur in Natang edition (original woodcut edition).

Dangyur in Zho'nyin edition.

Dangyur in Beijing edition (photo-offset copy of Tokyo University of Japan).

Tibet. It is composed of two parts: *Dangyur* and *Gangyur*. The latter includes sutrapitaka, vinaya-pitaka, abhidharma-pitaka, and supplementary canons. It records statements made by Sakyamuni, founder of Buddhism, and various Buddhist classics. It contains important materials related to ancient Indian history, philosophy and culture. *Dangyur*, meanwhile, collects annotations to *Gangyur* made by Indian and Tibetan scholars and translators of various generations. It is an encyclopedia with materials related to philosophy, literary, arts, language, astrology, calendar, medicine, industrial art, and architecture.

Woodblock printing gained ground during the Ming and ensuing dynasties. The Yongle edition of the Tripitaka was the first printed with woodblocks. After this, many monasteries in Tibet and Tibetan-inhabited areas in Sichuan, Qinghai and Gansu set up sutra print-ing houses. Many editions were printed, and the Yongle and some other editions are well preserved today. They including the following:

—Wanli edition: This was engraved with black ink in 1605 or the 33rd year of the reign of Ming Emperor Wanli, with blocks engraved in Beijing. Based on the Yongle edition, the Wanli edition contains 42-fold supplementary copies, bringing the number of folds to 150.

—Lijiang-Litang edition: This was engraved on the basis of the Chaba edition of *Gangyur* in 1609 or the 37th year of the reign of Ming Emperor Wanli. When Hoshod Mongols took the woodblocks to Litang, the Tripitaka printed with these woodblocks were called the Litang edition.

—Beijing edition: This was engraved in response to the edict of Qing Emperor Kangxi in 1683 or the 22nd year of the reign of Qing Emperor Kangxi, but its *Dangyur* woodblocks were engraved in 1724, or the second year of the reign of Qing Emperor Yangshan. It was, however, burnt in 1900 during the invasion of the Eight Powers.

—Zhonyi edition: This was engraved with woodblocks engraved in Zhonyi Monastery in Gannan in 1721, or the 60th year of Qing Emperor Kangxi. Its *Gangyur* woodblocks were engraved under the auspice of the 11th Headman Mosoi Gongbo; and its *Dangyur* woodblocks were completed under the auspice of the 14th Headman Zhonyi in 1753, or the 18th year of the reign of Qing Emperor Qianlong. This edition features complete content.

—Dege edition: This was engraved in 1729, or the 7th year of the reign of Qing Emperor Yongzheng, under the auspice of the 42nd Headman of Dege, Qoisoi Toinba Cering. More than 500 sutra block masters car-

Woodcut scripture cover of the Tibetan Tripitaka, Lhasa edition.

The *Gangyur* of Tripitaka in Tibetan, carved in 1921 and preserved in Muru Monastery, is the only woodcut Lhasa edition *Gangyur* of Tibet. It altogether includes 48,189 blocks contained in 100 cases. The picture shows a worker is sorting out the *Gangyur*.

ried out the work in five years. The Dege Headman died before the *Dangyur* blocks were completed, and his son completed the work.

—Natang edition: This was engraved in accordance with an instruction of the 6th Dalai Lama, Cayang Gyamco, and under the auspice of Dibo Sanggyi Gyamco. As the 6th Dalai Lama was demoted, the engraving work lasted 50 years until it was finally completed in 1741, or the 6th year of the reign of Qing Emperor Qianlong.

In addition, there are Lhagyia, Kulun, Potala, Qianlong, Lhasa, Qamdo, Labrang and some other editions of the Tripitaka.

During the period, Tibet saw the fast development of woodblock engraving and printing technology. And the sutras thus printed were spread to other parts of the world, and this in turn promoted the development of the Tibetan culture.

Qing High Commissioners and 29-Article Ordinance

During the Qing Dynasty (1644-1911), the Central Government exercised effective rule over Tibet. All the troubles confronting Tibet were solved thanks to efforts made by the Qing court. In 1724, the second year of the reign of Emperor Yongzheng, when the Qing court managed to suppress troubles plaguing Tibet, the court decided to send two High Commissioners to the region. Sengge and Malha were sent in 1727 to take in charge of Tibetan affairs. The 13-Article Ordinance for the More Effective Government of Tibet and the 29-Article Ordinance for the More Effective Government of Tibet all stipulated that the two High Commissioners would be in Tibet for a term of three years; they would handle Tibetan affairs together with the Dalai Lama and the Panchen Erdeni; they would take care of financial checks, supervision of judicial work, the training of local troops, and foreign affairs.

From 1727 to 1911, the Qing court dispatched 136 High Commissioners to Tibet. In addition to the above work, they sponsored the appointment and dismissal of local officials, and the incarnation and enthronement of the Dalai Lama, the Panchen Erdeni and all other Grand Living Buddhas. All these activities emphasized that they enjoyed the highest power in Tibet. The Gaxag, or the local government of

Gold urn bestowed by Emperor Qianlong of the Qing Dynasty. In 1793, Emperor Qianlong started the procedure of "drawing lot from the gold urn" when deciding the reincarnated boy of Dalai Lama, Panchen Erdeni and all other Grand Living Buddhas. For this purpose, he had two pure-gold urns made. They are 34 centimeters high. One of them is now enshrined in Potala Palace, and the other, in Yonghe Lamasery of Beijing.

Photo of British invaders when they arrived at Yadong region in 1904 (Front row, second from left, was Major General David MacDonald).

Tibet, was formed also with the efforts made by the High Commissioners.

No sign related to High Commissioners can be spotted in Tibet today, except for one place that is still called Dorsengge (Stone Lions), which derives its name from the fact that there were stone lions in front of the gate of the High Commissioner's Office.

In 1792, the Korgas invaded Tibet and the Qing emperor sent troops to drive them out. On the emperor's order, Qing General Fukang'an worked out a scheme to deal with problems confronting Tibet. The 8th Dalai Lama and the 7th Panchen Erdeni took part in working out the scheme and agreed that they would implement it after its approval by the emperor.

Together with the local officials in Tibet, General Fukang'an drafted the 29-Article Ordinance for the More Effective Governing of Tibet, which passed through the Qing court in 1793. It contained articles

related to rules and regulations to be followed, border defense, foreign negotiations, finance and trade, and the incarnation of Living Buddhas.

Castle on Dzong Hill of Gyangze where Tibetans fought against British invading troops.

Gunfire in 1904

Chinese and international historians agree that Tibet entered the modern era when the Tibetan people rose to resist the British invasion. Under the British threat, the Qing court signed the Sino-British Convention Relating to Burma in 1888, and the Anglo-Chinese Convention Relating to Sikkim and Tibet in 1890. The two unequal treaties brought harm to China.

In the 20th century, the British colonialists became unscrupulous in invading Tibet when they had won political and economic prerogatives there. The British Indian Viceroy, Lord Curzon, wrote a letter to the 13th Dalai Lama trying to negotiate with Tibet without the involvement of the Central Government.

43

However, the 13th Dalai Lama told the British he would not contact any foreigners without the consent of the Central Government. In this situation, Curzon planned the invasion of Tibet.

In 1904, British troops advanced from India into Tibet. In March, some 1,000 Tibetan soldiers and civilians rushed to confront the invaders in Qoimishango. The leader of the British force, Younghusband, played tricks by proposing negotiations. When the Tibetans came, he ordered his troops to open fire, killing some 500 Tibetans in a few minutes.

The slaughter angered the Tibetans. On April 9, the Tibetans, armed only with simple weapons, in Zachang, routed a mounted British detachment. British reinforcements rushed to the spot. Under the cover of rifle and machine-gun fire, they beat back the Tibetans and seized Gyangze, a town of strategic importance. Tibetan soldiers, civilians and monks gathered in the town and the two sides fought fierce battles. The Tibetan side recaptured Zongshan Castle and Younghusband narrowly escaped death during a night raid. However, the Tibetan side lost the battle over a period of three months, when the British invaders cut off water supply and because of some other reasons.

On July 14, General MacDonald led some 4,000 British troops to advance from Gyangze to Lhasa. When the British invaders were approaching the city, the 13th Dalai Lama fled under the cloak of darkness rather than faced having to sign any treaty with the invaders. The British captured Lhasa on August 3.

The 10th Panchen Erdeni Qoigyai Gyamcain supported the central government and hoped to liberate Tibet as early as possible.

On September 7, the local government of Tibet was forced to sign the Lhasa Convention with the British invaders. According to the unequal treaty, Tibet should not give any land and mineral resources to any other foreign countries, as it was within the sphere of British influence; Tibet should pay indemnity to the British; Tibet should clear a passage from India to Gyangze and Lhasa; Tibet should open Yadong, Gyangze and Gardak as trading ports; Tibet should accept the 1890 Treaty and delineate its boundaries with Sikkim; Tibet should allow the British troops to be stationed in Yadong. The treaty failed to win the endorsement of the Chinese Central Government, so it was not legal. However, the British tried to force the Qing court to accept it. In 1906, the Qing court signed with the British the Anglo-Chinese Convention Relating to Sikkim and Tibet. Based on this, the British later enjoyed some prerogatives in Tibet.

This segment of history is known to all, and the bullet holes in the Gyangze castle are still there.

Deputies of Tibet local government: (from left: Sangpo Toinzin Tungzhub, Kemu Soinam Wangdui, Ngapoi Ngawang Jigmei, Tubdain Danda and Tubdain Lemoin).

Peaceful Liberation of Tibet in 1951

With the birth of the People's Republic of China, the Chinese people voiced their demand for the reunification of the motherland. A small number of people in the upper echelon of the ruling class in Tibet, however, stood for separation from China, despite the fact that Tibet has remained a part of China since the Yuan Dynasty. While the Tibetan separatists worked to expel people of the Han ethnic group in Tibet and to send a "goodwill mission" to the West, patriotic Tibet-

On May 23, 1951, pleni-potentiaries of the Chinese Central Government and the local Tibet government signed in Beijing the "Agreement on Peaceful Liberation of Tibet."

ans cabled the CPC Central Committee, Chairman Mao and Commander-in-Chief Zhu De, demanding them to send troops to liberate Tibet. The 10th Panchen Erdeni cabled Mao and Zhu in October 1949 for the liberation of Tibet. Ngapoi Ngawang Jigmei and some other Tibetan officials opposed the action of the 14th Dalai Lama in fleeing Tibet and stood for peace talks with the Central Government.

Considering the actual situation in Tibet, the Central Government decided to liberate Tibet by peaceful means. In May 1950, the Central Government proposed

10 terms for this purpose, but the proposal met with opposition from Regent Dagzha. This forced the PLA to fight the Qamdo battle on October 6, 1950. The PLA's success shocked the Tibetan rulers and forced the Regent to step down. On November 14, 1950, the 14th Dalai Lama came to power and on January 27 1951, he sent a letter to the Central Government informing it of his willingness to negotiate with the Central Government for peace. He dispatched a team to Beijing thereafter.

The 5-member peace talks team was led by Ngapoi

On May 23, 1951, pleni-potentiaries of the Chinese Central Government and the local Tibet government signed in Beijing the "Agreement on Peaceful Liberation of Tibet."

Ngawang Jigmei and its members included Kemo Soinam Wangdui, Tubdain Danda, Tubdain Lemoin, and Sangpo Toinzhub. They reached Beijing on April 22 and 26, and the negotiations began on the 29th. Through six rounds of talks, both agreed on the 17 Articles of the Agreement for Methods for the Peaceful Liberation of Tibet. The Agreement stated that the local government of Tibet should get rid of imperialist influence and assist the PLA to enter Tibet; the Central Government to handle the foreign affairs of Tibet; Tibetan troops to be reorganized into the PLA; a lenient policy be followed in Tibet for the retention of the existing system; the Dalai Lama to continue to exercise his political and religious powers; the Tibetans should enjoy freedom of religious belief. A signing ceremony was held in Zhongnanhai, Beijing on May 23, 1951.

Ngapoi reported to the Gaxag government upon his return to Tibet. On October 24, the 14th Dalai Lama cabled Chairman Mao Zedong stating that he fully supported the Agreement.

Samye Monastery -- the first monastery combining Buddha, dharma and monk in Tibetan history.

Development of Tibetan Buddhism

On a spring day in 1984, the wind was blowing hard as I went to the Central Institute for Nationalities for a lecture by Prof. Wang Furen on the *Outline of Tibetan Buddhism*. The professor has since passed away, but his lectures are still fresh in my mind.

By the time of the 8th Tubo King Rabajun, some 200 years after Buddhism first spread into Tibet in the 7th century, the Tubo state had made much headway in terms of social and economic development. Monasteries were built, and the king decided that each household must have one member as a monk, and every seven households must support one monk. Eminent monks and translators were invited to translate Buddhist scriptures and compile Tibet's first Sanskrit dictionary.

The nobles were unhappy to see the monks growing in strength. In 838, the King Rabajun was killed and this segment of history has found its way into the fresco in the Norbu

Tibetan Buddhism and Temporal and Religious Administration

Lingka. Darma, brother of the slain king, ascended the throne with support of the Bon religionists. He handled government affairs according to set rules and regulations. Supported by his minister Congboin, he decreed that all monasteries be closed, and statues of Buddha be burnt up or buried underground. On the monastery walls were painted pictures showing monks drinking and seeking fun in an abusive way. During that period, monks were forced to resume secular life, and work as butchers or hunters. Buddhist scriptures were either burnt up or sealed off. This meant the end of the spread of Buddhism in the area. At the end of this particular segment of history, the Tubo Kingdom died out. Four hundred years of chaos and separation ensued.

Exterior view of Qoide Monastery of Gonggar. It is one of the most famous monasteries of Sagya sect, with a history of more than 700 years.

But this was not the end of Buddhism in Tibet. Some Buddhists fled to Dorkang and Ngari, where they worked hard to spread Buddhist tenets. Adixa, Padmasambhava and some other famous monks were invited to lecture on Buddhism. With the support of local political forces, the two places became Buddhist centers. In 970, Tibetan Buddhism made its way from Dorkang and Ngari to U-Tsang, ushering in its revival and further development in Tibet.

Great sutra hall of Zezhol Monastery, Dengqen County. The Zezhol Monastery is one of the Bon religion monasteries of eastern Tibet with the largest scale and most followers. It can be traced back to 2,000-3,000 years ago.

Rongbo Monastery of the Nyingma (or Red) sect was built in 1899 at the foot of Mount Qomolangma. It is the highest monastery of the world.

Rise of Five Buddhist Sects

There were many reasons for the comeback of Buddhism. The most important is that Buddhism actually merged with local forces although it met with suppression after 200 years of development. Some newly rising forces turned to support Buddhism. This nurtured the rise of the five Buddhist sects, the Nyingma, Sagya, Gedang, Gagyu and Gelug. Leaders of these sects played an important role in Tibetan history.

Nyingma Sect: Born in the 12th century, this sect was the oldest in Tibetan Buddhist. Nyingma means old and ancient. Its members declared that they propagated classics left behind from the Tubo period and worshipped Padmasambhava as their master. As the sect members wore red hats, the Tibetans nicknamed it the Red Sect. In the beginning, the sect was free from any monastery, monk organization and systematic sect doctrines. Buddhist tenets were passed among its members orally. Hence, others did not respect. The situation didn't change until later when three masters emerged and monasteries were built. The most important of the Nyingma monasteries were those in Dorjezha, Mingzhuling and Getu. The sect respects the secret school approach and looks down on the open school. This is why it lacked a system guiding monks to study. They did labor and could have wives and children. The sect was never able to form a monastic force.

Gedang Sect: "Ge" means Buddhist statement and "dang" means teaching. This sect was founded in the 11th century by Zongdainba, disciple of Adixa, according to his instruction. In 1055, Zongdainba presided over the mourning ceremony for his deceased master in Nyetang, and had a monastery built there. The Gedang Sect had its base set up in the monastery. Zongdainba had three disciples. While one of the three refused to take any disciples, two others--Bodorwa and Chinwowa--did their best to gain more students. The two developed their own sub-sects, with one teaching classics and the other featuring teaching by masters. When Bodorwa gave lectures, thousands of people attended. As a result, the Gedang Sect gained fame in U-Tsang. The sect advocated that sect members should study progressively and pay close attention to monastic rules and organizations. Its monasteries were found throughout Tibet. After the 12th century, it joined hands with local forces in Jorwo, Yarlung, Shannan, forming

Exterior view of Dalung Monastery of Lhunzhub. It was built in 1180. Under the Pagmo Zhuba Gagyu branch, it is called Dalung Gagyu sect.

Exterior view of Zhoimalhakang in Quxu. It was built in the 11th century when Adixa was spreading Buddhism. After the Parinirvana of Adixa, a stupa was built for him here.

a formidable force. However, as it failed to gain political power, it was no match for the Sagya and Gelug sects, which appeared later, in terms of political and administrative power. After the 15th century, Zongkapa founded the Gelug Sect on the basis of the Gedang Sect, and monks and monasteries all came under control of the new sect.

Sagya Sect: Sagya means "while clay"in Tibetan, This sect was founded by Gongqoigyi within the Kun clan, claiming to be offspring of the Tubo royal family. The sect derived its name from the Sagya Monastery. Legend has it that the ground on which the monastery was built was grayish white in color. The sect did its best to take students and as a result gained its influence quickly. Of the five masters beginning with Gonggarningbo, son of Gongqoigyi, and ending with Pagba, the 4th master Sapan Gonggar Gyaincain was the first to establish political ties with the Mongols and the 5th master Pagba was the first Imperial Tutor of the Yuan Dynasty. In the mid-14th century, the Sagya Sect was replaced by the Pagmo Zhuba regime before the Yuan made way for the Ming Dynasty. Nonetheless, it was still formidable in strength.

Gagyu Sect: The sect boasted more sub-sects than any others. It was strong until the emergence of the Gelug Sect. Gagyu means the oral spread of Buddha's statement. Two major sub-sects worked hard for this from its early days: the Tabo Gagyu founded by Marba, Milha Riba, and Tabo Lhagyie; and the Shanba Gagyu founded by Qoinbu Nanjor. While the Shanba Gagyu exerted less influence in its later days, the Tabo Gagyu branched out into eight sub-sects of four major schools: the Garma Gagyu, Chaba Gagyu, Barong Gagyu, and Pazhub Gagyu. Of the four sub-sects, the Pazhub Gagyu was the strongest. It had members who replaced the Sagya regime to rule the region and won honorific titles from the Central Government in the Central Plains. The Pagmo Zhuba later branched into eight small branches: Zhigong Gagyu, Dalong Gagyu, Zhuba Gagyu, Yasang Gagyu, Chopo Gagyu, Xiusai Gagyu, Yeba Gagyu, and Macang Gagyu.

The Garma Gagyu Sect was so influential that the Ming emperor granted the highest-ranking honorific title of Great Treasure Prince of Dharma to its chief

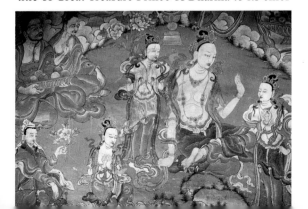

Mural of Samye Monastery: expounding the texts of Buddhism.

leaders, and bestowed them with a red hat and a black hat. The Black Hat Sect made the Curpu Monastery its main residence, and the tradition is still cherished today. It was the Garma Gagyu Sect that initiated the system of the reincarnation of Living Buddhas.

In the 15th century Zongkapa emerged. Born in Huangzhong, Qinghai, he studied Buddhist scriptures from eminent monks with the Sagya and Gagyu Sects. In 1409, he donated what he owned to build the Gandain Monastery, and founded the Gelug Sect. Zongkapa stood for religious reform featuring tight monastic rules including one that all monks had to wear a yellow hat so as to distinguish from other sects. Hence, the Gelug is also called the Yellow Sect. His disciples later built the Drepung, Sera, Tashilhungpo, Tar and Labrang monasteries, which are known as the six major monasteries of the Yellow Sect. In the 17th century, the Yellow Sect gained absolute power in Tibet, putting an end to fights for power among various Buddhist sects.

Summing up this segment of history, Pro. Wang Furen said: Tibetan Buddhism has, since its original emergence, integrated closely with the feudal serf owners; local feudal forces managed to control the Buddhist sects as they emerged and developed; therefore, Buddhist sects are related to culture, but even more to politics. Fights among these sects are in fact fights for political power.

Reincarnation of Living Buddhas

Xalhu Monastery of Xigaze was built in 1087. The monastery combines the Tibetan and Han building styles and is a cultural relic institution under the state-level protection.

Overall view of Drepung Monastery, the most important one of the six monasteries of the Gelug (or Yellow) sect.

The reincarnation of Living Buddhas, in essence, originated in the monastic economy. According to the *Blue Annals*, Abbot Garma Pakshi of the Curpu Monastery was the third-generation disciple of Marba, founder of the Gagyu Sect. He had 7,000 disciples and built the Garma Dainsa and Curpu monasteries, founding the Garma Gagyu Sect. As Master Duisum Qenba wore a black hat, the sect became known as the Black Hat Sect. In 1283, Garma Pakshi was about to pass away. All of a sudden, he opened his eyes and rose to sit on his folded legs. He summoned his disciple Wogyiba and told him in clear-cut words: "I will leave temporarily. After my departure, there will be one in a far-away place called Lhadui, who is the successor of the Black Hat. Before he comes, you will serve as the agent of Buddha."

He took off his gold-rimmed Buddha hat, put it on Wogyiba's head, and he passed away.

A boy was born in Gongtang, hometown of Milha Riba, Chief Master of the Gagyu Sect, in 1284. Five years later, he was determined as the soul boy of Garma Pakshi. The first reincarnated soul boy in Tibetan his-

Exterior view of Gandain Monastery, Dagze. Built in 1409, it is one of the six famous monasteries of the Gelug sect.

tory was greeted to the Curpu Monastery in 1289 and given the religious name Shianjoin Dorje, studying Buddhist doctrines from Wogyiba.

According to the *Blue Annals*, when the soul boy reached Curpu Monastery, Wogyiba had a high seat set up in the Sutra Hall and declared that this was prepared for Master. When the boy reached the monastery together with his parents, he went up to the high seat and sat on it. Astonished to see this, Wogyiba asked the boy why he sat on the Master's seat. The boy answered: "I am your Master!" Recalling what the Master had said on his deathbed, Wogyiba accepted the boy as the incarnate of his Master.

Reincarnation of a Living Buddha constitutes a major contribution Garma Gagyu made to Tibetan Buddhism. Prior to this, there were two major methods for selecting successors to the deceased masters: One was for the father to find his successor from among his children or in his own clan; the other was for a master to find his successor among his disciples. The Nyingma Sect selected a successor to the deceased master from among his children or in his own clan. The Minzhuling and Dorjezha monasteries beside the Yarlung Zangbo River were resident monasteries of the Nyingma Sect. This sect allowed its members to marry, and for sons to take up the mantles of their fathers. From the 16th to the mid-17th centuries, the two monasteries featured fathers passing the mantle on to their sons or sons-in-law. This is also the case for the Minzhuling Monastery today.

The Sagya Sect featured finding successors from the same clans. Gonggar Nyingbo, the first-generation abbot of the sect, was succeeded by his second son Kansoi Nanzemo. When Kansoi died, he gave his throne to his brother, Kanzha Batsang. When Kanzha passed away, the power fell to his nephew, Sagya Gonggar Gyaincain, who, in turn, made his nephew, Pagba, his own successor. Pagba, the fifth-generation abbot of the Sagya Sect, won the honorific title of Imperial Tutor from Yuan Emperor Kublai Khan, making it possible for the Sagya Sect to rule Tibet.

Zongdainba, the founding abbot of the Gedang Sect, had many disciples. He built the Razheng Monastery. Upon his death, his role was taken on by his disciple, Gongbawa. Masters of future generations followed his example in finding successors.

The Living Buddha reincarnation system was pio-

Great sutra hall of Sera Monastery of Lhasa. Firstly built in 1419, it is one of the most famous monasteries of Gelug sect.

Coqen Hall of Sera Monastery.

neered in the 13th century against the background that various Buddhist sects rose alongside with the construction of monasteries. The monastic economy gained ground. Some of the monasteries owned not only land, animals and pasturelands, but also subjects. For political and economic reasons, various sects were locked in fighting. In order to survive, their masters carefully chose their successors. The Dorjezha and Zhigung monasteries of the Nyingma Sect all adopted the new system.

The system was perfected by the Gelug Sect, founded in the 15th century. All of its monasteries adopted the system. Throughout the years, they followed a whole set of rituals and historical precedence in this regard.

Since 1653 when the 5th Dalai Lama received a title from the Qing Emperor Shunzhi, the system of Dalai Lama being conferred a title has been set up. The picture shows the gold certificate and gold seal used in conferring the title.

Reincarnation of the Dalai and the Panchen

Hundreds of Living Buddha reincarnation systems emerged in Tibet. Statistics show Grand Living Buddhas were called Hutogtu when they received their official titles from the Central Government or local authorities. During the Qing Dynasty (1644-1911), 160-odd Grand Living Buddhas were appointed Hutogtu and registered with the Commission for the Mongolian and Tibetan Affairs. Of these, the Dalai Lama and the Panchen Erdeni were the most influential, as they got their titles from the Central Government.

The Dalai Lama title emerged in 1576, when Soinam Gyamco of the Drepung Monastery went to lecture on Buddhism in Mongolia on the invitation of Tumet Mongol Chief Shunyi. Out of his respect for Soinam Gyamco, the chief granted him the honorific title of

Lamas blow religious horns at a ceremony of the Qambaling Monastery of Qamdo.

"Dalai Lama", a Mongolian word meaning "ocean" or "major master." Given the fact that Soinam Gyamco had two predecessors, he was the 3rd Dalai Lama, although he did not enjoy the level of power of later generations.

In 1652, the 5th Dalai Lama went to pay homage to Qing Dynasty emperor in Beijing, and the Qing emperor granted him the title officially and issued him a gold certificate of appointment and a gold seal of authority. From then on, the Dalai Lama gained his religious position in Tibet, a position no others can match.

The title of Panchen was granted by Hoshod Mongol Gushi Khan. In 1642, Gushi Khan wiped out the hostile forces of the Gelug Sect, and turned the political power over to the 5th Dalai Lama. Three years later, he granted Lobsang Qoigyi with the Tashilhungpo Monastery the title of "Panchen" and put the Xigaze area under his rule. Lobsang Qoigyi was the 4th Panchen. This was the source of the title of the Panchen which means major scholar in Mongolian. In 1713, the Qing court sent its envoy to the Tashilhungpo Monastery, granting Lobsang Qoigyi the honorific title of "Panchen Erdeni" and issued him a gold sheet of appointment and gold seal of authority. Henceforth, the Panchen Erdeni gained his position equivalent to that of the Dalai Lama politically and religiously.

Mr. Donggar on Temporal and Religious Administration

The temporal and religious administration in Tibet is different from any other system that combines government with religion in the West. Mr. Donggar, of Tibet University, achieved a lot in studying this segment of Tibetan history. According to his

Qamba statue (at the age of eight) worshipped on the 3rd floor of the great hall of Drepung Monastery. Drepung Monastery was built in 1416 and is the most important one of the six monasteries of the Gelug (or Yellow) sect.

understanding, the system is the best reflection of the relationship between the Central Government and the local government of Tibet. The temporal and religious administration came to an end in 1959 when the 14th Dalai Lama fled abroad after the armed rebellion was put down and the Gaxag government of Tibet was disbanded.

Gradually, a temporal and religious administration emerged with the endorsement of the Central Government, with the Dalai Lama being the religious leader and, at the same time, government leader. Its law was the monastic rules and the upper-class religious figures enjoyed supreme power.

As a matter of fact, when religion merges with po-

Palkor Monastery is home to Sagya, Gedain and Gelug sects of the Tibetan Buddhism.

litical power, the former will inevitably go downhill. After the 17th century, the Gelug Sect ruled Tibet and some other major sects such as Nyingma, Sagya and Gagyu, who had enjoyed power for some time, had to win the support of the new Gaxag government. At this

Sutra debate.

point of time, Buddhism is no longer a belief; it is a part of the political dictatorship. Poverty-stricken peasants and herders were tonsured to monasteries in large numbers. Many others, who sought officialdom, turned to the monasteries, too. In modern times, imperialists and separatists poked their noses into Tibet, disrupting normal religious life and social stability. With contradictions going from bad to worse, Tibetan Buddhism lost an environment for further development.

End of the 14th Dalai Regime in 1959

In 1951, Tibet won peaceful liberation, but continued to follow the old system. In July 1957, a religious ritual geared to "present the Dalai Lama with a gold throne" was held in the Potala Palace, and the public saw this as a move to pledge loyalty to the temporal and religious administration. This was followed by the organization of the so-called "religion protection army" though this went against Buddhist tenets.

Display of Buddha at the Drepung Monastery.

At about 8 March 10, 1959, some in Lhasa ran in the streets, crying: "Go to the Norbu Lingka! The Dalai Lama will be kidnapped by the Han!" The Norbu Lingka was besieged tightly.

Later, Ngapoi Ngawang Jigmei recalled:

"According to the Tibetan tradition and custom, on the 29th day of the 12th Tibetan month each year, the Sorcerer's Dance is held in the Potala Palace. On that day in 1959, only political commissar Tan Guansan and deputy commander of the Tibet Military Command Deng Shaodong were in Lhasa. Deng Shaodong and Guo Xilan, secretary of the Tibet Work Committee were invited to go to the Potala Palace. The 14th Dalai Lama met them in his living chamber. The 14th Dalai Lama told them to arrange the Tibet Song and Dance Ensemble to perform in the Auditorium of the PLA Tibet Military Area as the Norbu Lingka lacked necessary illuminating equipment.

"At about 3 on March 9, 1959, Li Zuomin, head of the United Front Work Department of the Tibet Work

Committee, told me at my home what was in the mind of the 14th Dalai Lama, and relayed what he said: Gaxag government officials may gather in the Norbu Lingka before going to the performing site together with him. I was afraid there would be something unexpected to happen, and told Li about this. Li said there was no way to change the plan. At seven that day, I received a call from Acting Galoon Liuxa Tubdain Taba, saying that the 14th Dalai Lama was to watch

Nyima Cering, lama of the Jokhang Monastery, is deeply loved by both Chinese and overseas visitors as a tour guide.

performance in the Auditorium of the PLA Tibet Military Area, and all the Galoons were to gather in the Norbu Lingka at nine.

"I had to preside over a study meeting on the morning of March 10, so waiting for call from the Norbu Lingka. At about 10, Sangpo Cewang Renzin, deputy commander of the PLA Tibet Military Area and commander-in-chief of the Tibetan army, rode to the Norbu

Monk of the Drepung Monastery.

Lingka directly. He was ambushed at a spot not far from the destination and was rushed to the clinic of the Indian consulate in Lhasa. After 10, Kamqoin Soinam Gyamco, brother of Parbalha Geleg Namgyi, was killed in front of the Norbu Lingka by rebels, and his body was tied to the galloping horse saddle. As the 14th Dalai Lama could not go to watch the performance, I went to the Tibet Military Area.

"This was what happened then. I am sorry there are still many Tibetan compatriots who are misled by rumors."

Facts uncovered later show that the 14th Dalai Lama played double-faced tricks to hoodwink the public. In doing this, he meant to protect the temporal and religious administration which had lasted for some 600 years. However, when he fled overseas, the Gaxag government was declared disbanded and the old system came to an end.

Display of Buddha at the Tashilhunpo Monastery.

Emancipated serfs met to urge a democratic reform as early as possible (1959).

Tibetan Serfdom Described by Foreigners

To understand past Tibetan society, it is necessary to understand serfdom. For this reason, I read widely. Here are some of the books I have read:

Ancient Tibet Faces New-Born China by Alexander D. Nell, a French Tibetologist, said that in old Tibet, all the peasants were slaves groaning under heavy debts throughout their life. They had to pay exorbitant taxes and undergo corvee labor, "losing personal freedom and becoming poor and poorer."

Poverty-stricken serfs and slaves turned to usury. The debt mounted year by year, so that none could escape. When they died, their children took over the debt....

They were paid nothing to work for the old Tibetan government and government officials who passed through their locality. They were not allowed to leave their hometown. Those who fled home would be returned to be beaten and forced to pay heavy fines; their relatives would also be beaten.

Describing the situation, American anthropologists M.C. Gorcedan and

Democratic Reform and Self-Government in Tibet

Part of articles of the Code of Thirteen Rules of Procedure and Punishment worked out by Tibet local government.

70

Wooden shackles in prisons of old Tibet could cuff four to five "prisoners" each.

Z.M. Bill pointed out in their *Tibetan Herdsmen Today--Tibet in American Eyes* that the Tibetan system benefited from forcing the labor force to work for manorial lords. Herders attached to manors were not allowed to leave under any circumstances. This made it possible for religious circles, the government and those in the upper ruling class to gain cheap, indentured labor. In essence, the Gaxag government in Lhasa owned the land. For hundreds of years, however, the noble families, Grand Lamas or monasteries controlled the land. Such a system was very much like that in Middle Ages Europe, Tsarist Russia and feudal Japan.

In his *Portraits of Tibet*, David MacDonald said that when one inmate was to be executed, he/she would be put into a leather bag and thrown into a river. The leather bag floated on water for five minutes until it sank. Then, the dead felon was fished out and dismembered, the parts being thrown back into the river. In other cases, limbs were amputated, eyes gouged out or hot oil or water poured into the eyes. Inmates who survived all these would be thrown into a dark, wet, filthy den unsuitable for human habitation. Other punishments included being shackled heavily, whipped 1,000 times....

It was described in the *Biography of the 13th Dalai Lama* that whipping was common occurrence. The accused would be whipped, and those who accused the offenders and even the eyewitnesses would be whipped, too. Iron shackles were applied to the killers and thieves. Those who murdered others would be put into a leather bag and thrown into the river until they

Too heavy to bear -- woman serf of suburban Lhasa was carrying wheatgrass back.

died; those who robbed would have their noses or hands cut off; those who committed political crimes would have their eyes gouged out.

Zongboin and other local executives were empowered to whip the accused so long as death did not occur. Though most of people committed theft did so out of poverty, they were severely punished. Some had their noses, fingers cut off, while some others had their eyes gouged out, so that shackled blind people begging for a living in the street were seen everywhere in Lhasa.

Some other international writers said that Tibet was free from economically formidable middle class; monks and lamas controlled the manorial lords. As the Tibetans were very religious, monks and lamas were so powerful that even Living Buddhas could do nothing without their help.

Li Youyi's Description of Tibet in the Late 1940s

Li Youyi was director of the General Affairs Office of the Tibet Office of the KMT Commission for Mongolian and Tibetan Affairs. Later on, he was known as

Serfs must do corvee labor regularly for their lords. In harvest season, they had to give up work on their own land but worked for the lords. The picture is a record of a serf's labor. He could get a seal mark from the butler once he worked for one day.

Serfs and slaves did a forced labor -- twisting woolen yarn -- for their lord Surkang Wangqen Geleg in Kaisong Manor of Shannan.

a famous Tibetologist and now lives in the United States.

In his book titled *Tibet: The Mysterious Vs The Not Mysterious*, Mr. Li said that he did an investigation in Tibet in 1945 and traveled along the Yarlung Zangbo River for 1,700 miles. He was discouraged by the devastation of deserted dwellings and abandoned fields. He talked to people he encountered and they were ignorant of World War II.

An old serf, aged over 80, still worked for her owner -- making butter.

"When I was in a Nyingchi village, I came across an old lady. I asked her something about the village ahead, but she said she had never been there. Actually, it was only two or three kilometers away. Slaves and serfs had to toil in the fields, and they had no time to visit others close to them."

Mr. Li went on to say that, although the Tibetans were addicted to buttered tea, not all of them had access to it. Those in dire poverty didn't have money to buy any sort of tea, not to mention buttered tea. "During my investigation, I came across people who had been drinking Baigyia tea composed of tree bark and leaves and Bamgyia tea which was actually a kind of moss. Tea made with such tea substitutes was free from any sort of tea taste."

According to Mr. Li, the Tibetans ate *zanba* (roasted highland barley flour), but the serfs could not have it every day. When the rent was paid after the autumn harvest, little remained. People had to borrow food and their debt mounted high and higher. Sometimes, they had to resort to wild herbs. Mr. Li asked them why they did not rise up in rebellion, they refused, saying their treatment was due to sins they perpetrated in their previous life. They believed in what the lamas told them. In this sense, the religious opium is more horrible than mere punishment, as the latter would encourage rebellion, but the former made the serfs and slaves obedient and submissive to their poor life.

Democratic Reform and Emancipation of Serfs

Under the feudal serfdom, serfs and slaves made up 95 percent of the Tibetan population, but owned nothing. Serf owners who made up only less than 5 percent of the population, however, owned 95-odd percent of the wealth. In 1959, the Tibetan society had made certain progress. Unable to accept changes, some

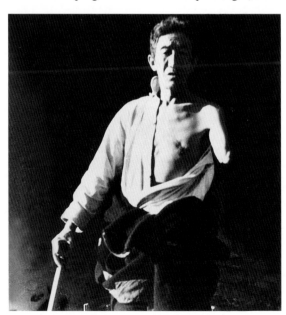

An impoverished serf had to have his left arm cut because he could not pay his owner enough taxes.

in the upper ruling class staged an armed rebellion, killing people who favored such social changes. When the rebellion was put down, the 14th Dalai Lama took them abroad where they organized a government in exile. This put an end to the enforcement of the serfdom which still held sway after the peaceful liberation of Tibet in 1951, and made it possible for the Central Government to decide to conduct the Democratic Reform ahead of time.

Tibetan children vied for food with wild dogs.

During the Democratic Reform that lasted from 1959 to 1960, the million serfs won emancipation and became masters of their society. They were given land to till and houses to live in. In the autumn of 1960, some 364,000 kg of grain converted from usury was declared as "not to be paid"; the serfs and slaves harvested some 28 million kg of grain for self-consumption; and about 20,000 household servants were given 2.52 million kg of grain and settled down.

With food in stomach, the serfs and slaves sang: "With the Dalai, the sun shines over the nobility, but with Chairman Mao, the sun shines over us the poor; while the sun for the nobility has set, our sun rises."

The Democratic Reform proved to be very successful, with some 200,000 peasants issued with land deeds and winning freedom. Chen Zonglie, then a young men, recorded the segment of history with cameras, and photos taken then are touching and moving.

Historians recorded the history this way:

On June 28, 1959, the Preparatory Committee for the Founding of the Tibet Autonomous Region held

Cering Zhoima, a serf of Surkang Wangqen Geleg, was driven out of the manor as she got old. She had to live on begging and sleep in a water toilet.

its second session, adopting the Resolution on Conducting the Democratic Reform in Tibet and the Methods on Rent and Interest Reduction in the Tibetan Areas. According to the new rule, debts the serfs and slaves borrowed from the serf owners before 1958 were declared null and void, while debts borrowed in 1959 were to be paid at a reduced interest rate. During its third session, it was decided to abolish feudal serfdom and distribute land among the tillers, and adopted the Methods Concerning Reform of the Land System in Tibet. In December 1959, it was decided that herd owners were not allowed to fire tenants at will.

Diary on Democratic Election in Tibet

Diaries of Lin Tian is obviously a good book for readers to gain a better understanding of the progress of the Democratic Reform. Lin is a journalist who worked in Tibet in the late 1950s. The book recorded his experience there in 1960:

The meeting began. Everyone raised their head, with mouth open, to listen to the sort of speeches never heard before. Comrade Zhang with the Work Team took the floor first: "Today, the sufferers and the oppressed meet for the first time. What is the meeting about? You know your master Soikang was involved in the rebellion, but has run away....One of you will be elected to lead oth-

A slum area of Lhasa before the Democratic Reform.

ers to live a new life. But, who should be elected? Can this person be unlettered? Can it be a woman? Yes! So long as he or she can win trust from others."

At this point, the people had broad smiles on their faces. Nyima Cering was finally elected. The sun-tanned man had been working for the Kaisum Manor for 15 years ever since his father died when he was nine. A girl who was a household servant was elected deputy chief. All the others were either household servants or serfs.

A panel discussion was held in three groups. "Neighbors and friends," said an old man with mustache and deep wrinkles in his face, "Those who have been elected are not there to oppress us and curse us. Instead, they are to lead us onto a road to better life. I witnessed how they suffered in old society. They will not forget us."

Serfs escaping from Nyemo to Lhasa had to sleep on the street.

Former household servants thanked the CPC and the Central Government for giving them freedom and a better life.

When it was the turn for the elected leaders to speak, Nyima Cering said: "It is Chairman Mao Zedong and the CPC who have emancipated us. Since I am elected, I will work hard in your interest."

National Regional Autonomy

In the early days of the founding of the People's Republic of China in 1949, the Central Government promulgated policies for national regional autonomy, which found their way into the Common Program adopted at the 1949 CPPCC National Committee and also the 1954 PRC Constitution. As one of the regions dominated by ethnic minorities, Tibet followed the system.

It is stipulated in the 17-Article Agreement for the peaceful liberation of Tibet, signed on May 23, 1951, that Tibet enjoys the right to exercise national regional autonomy under the centralized leadership of the Central People's Government. In April 1956, the Preparatory Committee for the Founding of the Tibet Autonomous Region was set up, with the 14th Dalai Lama serving as the director, the 10th Panchen Erdeni the first deputy director and PLA General Zhang Guohua the second deputy director. Ngapoi Ngawang Jigmei was its secretary general.

In March 1959, those in the upper ruling class in

Prisoners of old Tibet could not get food at all. The two "prisoners" with shackles on had to go begging on street.

Farmers got certificates for their own land in 1960 after the Democratic Reform.

Tibet staged an armed rebellion, and the office building of the Preparatory Committee, which did a lot for the Tibetans, was attacked by the rebels. This forced the State Council to disband the former government of Tibet known as Gaxag, and the Preparatory Committee took over the ruling power; when the 14th Dalai Lama was not holding the post, the 10th Panchen Erdeni served as the director.

In September 1965, the Tibet Autonomous Region was founded. A total of 301 delegates attended the conference, including 242 who are of the Tibetan, Hui, Moinba and Lhoba ethnic groups. They included emancipated serfs and slaves, patriots on the upper religious and political classes. Through democratic election, Ngapoi Ngawang Jigmei was elected chairman of the People's Congress of the Tibet Autonomous Region; and Zhou Renshan, Pagbalha Geleg Namgyia, Guo Xilan, Xirab Toinzhu, Namdain Gonggar Wangqug, Cuike Toinzhub Cering, and Sengqen Lobsang

Gyaincain were elected vice-chairmen.

The key to the system of national regional autonomy lies in the fact that people in the region are masters of their own fate, enjoying various rights including the right to vote and the right to stand for vote. From 1979 to 1999, six democratic elections were held. During the democratic election held in 1993, 1,311,085 people, or 57 percent of the Tibetan population, were registered voters. 1,200,914 of them, or 91.6 percent, voted. They elected 6,411 deputies to the county and township people's congresses, 450 deputies to the People's Congress of the Tibet Autonomous Region and 19 deputies to the PRC National People's Congress.

Through the democratic elections, a number of Tibetans mounted the political stage. They include six elected chairman of the government of the Tibet Autonomous Region and five chairmen of the People's Congress of the Tibet Autonomous Region. They are Ngapoi Ngawang Jigmei: Elected chairman of the People's Committee of the Tibet Autonomous Region in September 1965, and re-elected chairman of the regional government for the period April 1981-February 1983; Tianbao elected for the period August 1979-April 1981; Dorje Cedain elected as secretary of the CPC Tibet regional committee and chairman of the regional government for the period 1983-85; Dorje Cerang elected acting chairman and later chairman of the Tibet regional government for the period November 1985-May 1990; Gyaincain Norbu elected chairman of the Tibet regional government for three terms May 1990-March 1993, March 1993-1996, and 1996-

The enchanting Potala Palace

1999; and Leqoi was elected chairman of the Tibet regional government in 1999.

I was in Tibet in 1993, when the People's Congress of the Tibet Autonomous Region met in Lhasa. According to statistics I have collected, people's congresses in various areas in the region elected 1,264 town and township heads, 99.6 percent of them being Tibetan; 71 chairmen of the people's congresses of various areas, 97.18 percent of them being Tibetan; 72 county magistrates, 98.6 percent being Tibetan; and 14 vice-chairmen of the People's Congress of the Tibet Autonomous Region, 71.43 percent of them being Tibetan. Of the leaders at the regional government level, some came from poor families and some others from families of former serf owners. They include Gyipu Puncog Cedain who was manorial lord of the Gyipu Manor, and Lhaba Puncog who was a servant of that manor.

Dalai's So-Called High-Level Autonomy

Beautiful scenery of Zayu.

Tibet Agricultural and Pastoral Academy.

In the past 36 years since the founding of the Tibet Autonomous Region, great changes have taken place on the roof of the world. People enjoy increasingly better life and the Tibetan society enjoys peace and stability. More than two-thirds of the Tibetans have escaped from poverty and many of them have reached a well-to-do level. All these point up the fact that the system of the national regional autonomy is an ideal system to follow for the Tibetans.

Closing his eyes to the full rights enjoyed by the Tibetans, however, the 14th Dalai Lama talks glibly about "real autonomy" and "high-level autonomy". He even calls for enforcement of the "one country, two systems" as it is the case in Hong Kong and Macao.

The new sluice gate of Tanghe Hydropower Station in Xigaze, one of the 62 "Aid-Tibet Projects" provided by the central government and other provinces or cities.

The fact is that Hong Kong and Macao were under foreign rule, and Tibet remains under the Central Government. The "one country, two systems" policy is not applicable to Tibet as a result.

Talking about the so-called "real autonomy" and "high-level autonomy" demanded by the 14th Dalai Lama, many Tibetans say: "What? High-level autonomy? Oh, he is saying `my rule'!"

They also say: "The sun of the temporal and religious administration has set. Can it rise from the west? Definitely not!"

A farmer's house in Gyangze County is being painted.

Barkhor Bazaar of Lhasa.

Aftermath of the "Cultural Revolution"

No one in China can deny the fact that the chaotic "cultural revolution" was a disaster for China, Tibet included. Though located far from the inland areas, Tibet could not escape the conflagration.

While the Red Guards in the hinterland were working hard to "fight feudalism, capitalism and revisionism", those in Tibet directed their venom against Tibetan Buddhism. Some monks were forced to return to a secular life, sutra books were burnt down, and some monasteries were dismantled--actions now recognized by all as detestable and ignominious. While a small number of monasteries were protected by a special decree issued by the Central Government department concerned because of their unusual value, the majority were not so lucky.

Recalling that segment of history, one can hardly understand now such things could happen. It was a political movement in a crazy period, in

Reform Program Enjoys Popularity

which nothing was impossible. In the early 1950s, the Central Government enacted a series of policies regarding development of various undertakings and religion. However, the "cultural revolution" not only arrested progress but even acted as a retrograde force. At that time, some herders were made to grow crops and industrial enterprises with no access to raw materials were set up to create energy. Tibetan handicrafts, rooted deeply in Tibetan culture, were discarded as "capitalism."

In 1976, when the "cultural revolution" was officially declared over, its impact lingered on. To change the situation, the Central Government held a number of special conferences on work in Tibet in the ensuing years.

Two Work Conferences on Tibet in the Early 1980s

In March 1980, the CPC Central Committee held the First National Conference on Work in Tibet. Lasting from March 14-15, it was chaired by Hu Yaobang, then General Secretary of the CPC Central Committee, who carried out investigations in Tibet. He stressed that the Tibetan cadres and Tibetan people should play the major role under the new historical conditions; proceeding from the actual situation in Tibet, efforts should be made to cure the wounds caused by the "cultural revolution" and improve the region's standard of living. Efforts would be made to build a united, prosperous and culturally advanced Tibet.

Efforts had already been made to right the wrongs

perpetrated during the "cultural revolution" after the "gang of four" was arrested. However, the conference decided that Herculean efforts are still needed to clear up all problems left by history, reverse all past wrongs, and implement the Central Government policy for freedom of religious belief by finding jobs for some 1,000 religious figures, repairing and rebuilding monasteries and restoring religious festivals.

Students of Tibet Agricultural and Pastoral Academy are learning about electricity.

With regard to production, the Central Government adopted the policy of improving the life of farmers and herders by developing production and wiping out poverty. Beginning in 1980, it stopped collecting agricultural and livestock breeding taxes in Tibet with a view to alleviating the burden of farmers and herders, and to cover the funds needed by Tibetan children to attend primary schools. This policy was released on June 20 in the form of government decrees.

With regard to the 14th Dalai Lama, the Central

Xigaze No.2 Middle School, completed in 1995 with the aids from Shanxi Province and Dalian City, is one of the 62 "Aid-Tibet Projects".

Government announced he was welcomed to return home so long as he gave up his stand for "Tibetan independence" and stopped working for that purpose. Those who followed him abroad were welcomed to come back for a visit or for settlement. They were also free to come and go.

Within a few years, Tibet witnessed great changes, with many Tibetan overseas compatriots returning to settle down or to visit friends and relatives.

During the Second National Conference for Work in Tibet, it was decided that nine provinces and municipalities directly under the Central Government, including Beijing, Shanghai, Tianjin and Jiangsu, would undertake 43 turnkey construction projects in Tibet in the fields of energy, transport, cultural education, physical education, public health, commerce, tourism, public utility works. Major projects included the Yangbajain Geothermal Power Station, the renovation of the Lhasa Thermal Power Station, the water supply and drainage project in Lhasa, the Xigaze Solar Energy Experimental Power

Station, the No.1 People's Hospital of the Tibet Autonomous Region, the Mass Art Hall of the Tibet Autonomous Region, the Tibet Gymnasium, and the Lhasa TV Teaching Building.

In 1985, the 20th anniversary of the founding of the Tibet Autonomous Region, the 43 projects were completed and put into operation, bringing many changes to the plateau region.

Repair of Damaged Monasteries

The Central Government policy for freedom of religious belief was implemented after the two national conferences, leading to a revival of religious activities and the repair of monasteries.

The Grand Summons Ceremony in Lhasa was suspended in 1966. When it was restored on the Tibetan New Year's Day in 1986, tens of thousands of monks and lamas from the three major monasteries in Lhasa, and monasteries in the surrounding areas, gathered in Jokhang Monastery for the 21-day Ceremony. They

China-Nepal trade fair.

Lama of Nyainrong County in northern Tibet plateau is explaining to a pilgrimage herdsman the "magic power" of the solar energy the monastery uses.

met six times a day. Governments at various levels gave alms.

During the Grand Summons Ceremony, the tradition for lamas to take exams for Larangba Geshi academic degree was restored, and six lamas including Yexei Wangqug with the Sera Monastery succeeded in winning the highest Buddhist degree.

On the evening of the 15th day of the first Tibetan month, a butter lamp festival was held. On the 24th day, the statue of Qamba Buddha was carried along

The statue of Padmasambhava, founder of the Nyingma (or Red) Sect, and his footprint carved out of stone, are worshipped in the Lamaling Monastery of Nyingchi County.

Display of Buddha at the Potala Palace.

Barkor Street in Lhasa, signifying the end of the Grand Summons Ceremony.

Other religious festivals restored include the Qammo dance festival in Sagya Monastery, the Ximoqenbo Summons Ceremony in Tashilhunpo Monastery, the Walking Around the Holy Soul Rock Festival in the Razheng Monastery, the Todiqoiba dance festival in Samye Monastery, the Meidorqoiba Summons Ceremony in Caigongtang Monastery, and the sorcerer's dance festival in Curpu Monasery.

Thus far, the Central Government has earmarked some 200 million yuan to repair monasteries in Tibet including the Jokhang, Sera, Razheng, Curpu and Zhigung monasteries in the Lhasa area; Qambaling, Rawoqe and Zaya monasteries in the Qamdo area; Tashilhungpo and Palkor monasteries in Xigaze; Dorjezha, Mingzhuling, Sangding and Sanggar Gudor monasteries in Shannan; Llamaling Monastery in Nyingchi; Toding Monastery in Ngari; as well as the

Sutra debate at the grand praying ceremony.

Potala Palace and the Guge Kingdom Ruins. The repair of the Potala Palace in 1989 consumed some 52 million yuan, and the repair of the Gandain Monastery in October 1997 consumed 20 million yuan.

About 2,000 monasteries and other religious activity centers have been opened over the years, with over 40,000 resident monks and nuns. Many Tibetans have sutra halls or shrines set up at home. They are free to worship Buddha either at home or in monasteries.

I attended a holy dance festival in Qengpo, where many eminent monks practiced Buddhism in ancient times. Located at 4,300 meters on the slope of Narui Mountain, northeast of Samye Monastery, it attracted an endless flow of pilgrims and visitors with its 108 meditation caves.

I visited one of these caves shaped by two giant rocks like a triangle. Wooden planks were used to make the door. It enshrined the statue of Sakyamuni, founder of Buddhism. By the statue were tiny butter lamps, two bags of roasted highland barley flour, and one aluminum pot to be used to make tea.

According to Ranyima, a nun aged about 60, she had been there for seven years. "My parents died when I was young. I became a nun later, and have been to many places for worship. In the end I decide to spend my remaining years here," she said.

"I eat roasted highland barley and drink tea every day. That's all.

"When I have headache, which happens occasionally,

Tashilhunpo Monastery.

Grand summons cer-
emony of Lhasa.

I ask other nuns to fetch some medicine."

Some 100 meters away is another cave occupied by Raodain, aged 70. When his wife died, he left his two sons in Qamdo, and walked there to make his permanent home. His sons managed to find him and did their best to persuade the old man to come back home, but he refused to enjoy family happiness. "I have made vows in front of the statue of Buddha," he said. "How can I go back on my word?"

Raodain suffers from arthritis, and has difficulties moving around. "Fortunately, there are many pilgrims visit here," he said. "They bring me food and tea. I am lucky to stay in this area and wish to be buried here after my death."

Unlike these two, who live on alms, Chilai Puncog, 73, came from a rich family. With 6,000 yuan, he built a 20-square-meter sutra hall on the mountain slope for the protection of a nearby pagoda and also for meditation. He also spent 1,000 yuan to have a bronze statue of Padmasambhava cast. Unlike others, his sutra room was decorated with fresh flowers and sheep wool cushions. And he wore sheep wool monk robes and a wristwatch. He drank buttered tea while reciting sutras.

Rescuing Traditional Tibetan Culture

It has been claimed and repeatedly echoed in the West that Tibetan culture is being ruined. In fact, ever since the early 1980s, great efforts have been made to rescue ancient classics and traditional cultural relics. A case in point is *King Gesar*, an epic I have been studying for many years. The 100,000-line epic has been orally passed down through history. Rescuing it has been one of the major projects undertaken by the State ever since the 1980s, and special organs have been set up for the purpose. Registered epic singers total over 40 people, including Zhaba (an old artist) and Yumei (a young woman artist from Nagqu Grasslands). Gambian Gyamco, my tutor who specialized in the study of *King Gesar*, was the director of the Office of the King Gesar of the Chinese Academy of Social Sciences. Over two decades, they recorded thousands of tapes. Based on this, over 3 million copies in 100-plus volumes of *King Gesar* in Chinese were published. In addition, close to 100 articles and dozens of works, on the epic, were published. This proved to be an unprecedented cultural harvest in history.

Efforts made to gather and compile folk literature, opera, music and dance are also crowned with great success. Books published as a result include *Collected Folk Songs of Tibet*, *Collected Folk Stories of Tibet*, *Collected Folk Sayings of Tibet*, *Collected Tibetan*

Famous Tibetan balladeer Tubdain is narrating *King Gesar*.

A family of northern Tibet is celebrating the Tibetan New Year.

Music, Collected Tibetan Dances, and *Tibetan Operas.*

The Shoton (Sour Milk Drinking) Festival, the Ongkor (Harvest) Festival and some other traditional events have been restored, and become merged with the performance of Tibetan opera, song and dances, and sports activities. During the national ethnic minority sports meet in 1999, the Tibetans astonished everyone with their achievements in various traditional items.

Traditional Tibetan paintings and sculptures have also been restored and carried forward, and a good contingent of young artists is cutting a brilliant figure in these arts.

Organs set up for Tibetan studies now include eight research organs, including the Tibetan Academy of Social Sciences, and more than 20 research centers including the China National Center for Tibetan Studies in Beijing and the Sichuan Tibetology Center. They

Circling the farm fields during the Ongkor Festival.

The 11th Panchen Erdeni was giving blessing touch on the foreheads of disciples when an auspicious rainbow appeared above the palace.

have compiled and published more than 1 million volumes in some 300 kinds of Tibetan classics, and collated and published pattra-leaf sutras in Sanskrit. Symposiums and academic exchanges have been held for domestic and international Tibetologists. More than 10 kinds of journals, such as *Tibetan Research*, *Tibetology in China*, *China's Tibet*, *Tibet Folklore* and *Tibetan Buddhism* have been published.

In the last few years, State departments concerned have invested tens of million yuan to develop Tibetan medicine. Veteran Tibetan medicine doctors were or-

Performance of picking up hadas on a galloping horse, a program at the horse-racing fair of northern Tibet.

At the annual horse-racing fair of northern Tibet prairie, a new "tent city" will appear.

ganized to compile and publish up to 1 million volumes in some 20 kinds of classics on Tibetan medicine, including the *Collected Charts on the Four-Volume Medical Code*. Success has been achieved in standardizing the scientific analysis of traditional Tibetan medicine. Tibetan calendars are compiled on the yearly basis.

Lhasa Faces a New World

Lhasa, an ancient city, has, since the 1980s, made much headway in economic and social progress. I worked there for 10 years in the 1970s, and visited Xigaze, Shannan, Nyingchi, Qamdo and Nagqu. I knew what Lhasa was like then. When I visited Lhasa in 2000, I found a completely new city.

When the city of Lhasa was first built in the 7th century, major architecture included the Jokhang Monastery in the downtown area and the Potala Palace towering on the top of the Red Hills. The sole main street was the Barkor. Gradually, residences were built for noble families and Living Buddhas; and stores, workshops, markets, teahouses, wine shops and civil-

ian houses were also built to meet the need. After 1,
300 years of construction and reconstruction, the city
still covered only 3 square km. No modern streets and
public works were available in the early 1950s. Ram-
shackle paths were mined with hung excrement or
haunted by wild dogs, and large groups of starving
people, mere bags of bones, were reduced to begging.

Modern construction didn't start until in the 1960s,
and reached a high tide in 1964. Six streets in the
modern sense were built around the Potala Palace, including the 50,000-square-meter commercial street of

Dancer of "guozhuang"
in Qamdo is ladling out
highland barley wine for
people to quench their
thirst.

the People's Road, the Cultural Palace for the Laborers,
and the Lhasa Cinema. The PRC State Council ap-
proved a blueprint for building Lhasa into a historical
and cultural city of China. Of the 43 projects built in
Tibet in the 1980s with inland investments, 18 were
located in Lhasa; of the 62 aid projects built in Tibet
in the 1990s with inland investments, 17 were in Lhasa.

Lhasa today is a combination of the traditional and

modern, covered with greenery. Flanking the radiating modern streets are modern buildings and Tibetan-style architecture, city gardens and urban sculptures. Cultural relic units are well protected.

On June 1, 2000 or the 15th day of the fourth Tibetan month, the Sagya Dawa Festival was held. People donned their traditional best gathered at Lingkor Road to pray. Cashing in on this opportunity, business people

A handicraft market.

put up stands for business purpose. On Lingkor Road south, four young Tibetans fried and sold potato chips, attracting many to have a taste.

To the north of the Dragon King Pool were stalls offering daily necessities and garment decorations, plus food. One man from Sichuan sold hot peppers at a rate of 20 yuan per kg. As it was inexpensive by the local standard, his goods were sold up in a few hours. Cold German beer sold well there, too.

According to merchants of the Hui ethnic group in front of a mosque, sports shoes and sports sweaters

Foreign visitors dress themselves up in Tibetan clothes and go shopping with Tibetan woman (the middle).

enjoyed good sales.

One man from Santai County sold more than 500 balloons in half a day at 5 yuan each.

The three traditional ritual walking streets--Namkor, Barkor and Lingkor--were a scene of religious activities and modern business.

With modern streets emerging in the ancient city, motor vehicles increase in number. Traffic jams often occur. I cycled to the city's post office center and encountered a serious traffic jam, and was later told construction of the Potala Palace Square was in full swing, and all motor vehicles going that way had to bypass it.

Statistics show that there are seven taxi companies in Lhasa; they boast more than 700 taxis and over 500 mini-buses. In addition, there are close to 500 tricycle-cars. Locals love to ride motorcycles, and their number rivals those in the cities of Hainan and Guangdong. For a city with some 100,000 people, these vehicles constitute a formidable figure. No wonder there are traffic jams.

While a traffic jam is a city disease to be treated, it is new to Lhasa. Many national newspapers reported under the title of Traffic Jam Hits Lhasa for the First Time in History. Considering the situation in Lhasa, the problem represents progress in a way.

To the east of the Potala Palace is Zongjorlukang Market. Covering an area of 5,138 square meters, it has more than 1,200 stands offering a wide range of farm products and animal by-products and seasonings. The daily transaction value totals more than 800,000 yuan, and daily visitors number some 30,000. It supplies vegetables and non-staple food to half of the population of Lhasa, as well as to Shannan, Xigaze, Nagqu, Ngari and Nyingchi.

In the 1960s and 1970s, the Tibetans had supply of

Beijing Road with a facelift in Lhasa.

cabbages, turnips and potatoes only. Workers of Han ethnic group often brought back fruit and vegetables when they returned from visits to relatives in the hinterland. There is a well-known saying in Lhasa: "The rich eat vegetables, while the poor eat meat!"

Market supply is indeed ample today. Zongjorlukang plays an important role in this regard. In terms of supplies, it rivals those in Chengdu (Sichuan Province) and Kunming (Yunnan Province). It even offers bananas and oranges from south China, pears from north China, grapes from Xinjiang in west China, pineapples and mango from Guangxi, watermelons from Gansu and Qinghai provinces, as well as oranges from Nepal.

Former Tibetan shepherdess (the right) is now manager of a retail department of Bango County Cashmere Plant in Lhasa. Their cow cashmere sweaters find great popularity among customers.

Lhasa's Sense of Environmental Protection

Environmental protection is a topic much discussed

Vegetable market of Lhasa.

today in Lhasa. The fact is that Tibet remains clean. Statistics released in 1999 show that Tibet is the least polluted area in the world today, and the air is the cleanest.

Specialists hold that the roof of the world regulates the climate in the world, and Tibet is the source of many rivers famous in China and Southeast Asia. The content of sulfur dioxide in the air in Lhasa is 0.1 mg per cubic meters, less than the State stipulated standard. Despite a dense population in downtown Lhasa, the dust content in the air remains at less than 0.4 mg per cubic meters.

Thanks to efforts made to spread knowledge about environmental protection, some 20 people in Lhasa wrote jointly to the city government in 2000 complaining about pollution caused by the Lhasa Cement Works. The city government ordered an investigation, which led to the Cement Works being told to carry out renovation work or "close down." The Cement Works invested 3 million yuan in the renovation project and the problem was solved as a result. For a road con-

Come on to draw a lottery!

New vegetable market of Qamdo Town.

struction project carried out with an investment of 40 million yuan from Jiangsu Province, 700 popular trees would have to be felled. Local people asked whether these trees could be retained. Specialists with the City Bureau for Environmental Protection explained that popular trees are not a good tree specie for the city; flanking the new road will be willows and snow pines that beautify the environment.

Basum Co of Nyingchi boasts a picturesque scenery and elegant environment.

In the last few years, much headway has been made to protect wildlife in Tibet. Long-tail monkeys, not found for years, appear in the forested areas in Yadong; river deer now are bold enough to seek food down the mountains; red-billed gulls have settled in the Dragon King Pond Park; and wild donkeys are too many to cope with in Ngari, forcing the locals to ask the local government to wipe out some. Out of the need for the protection of wildlife, the local government refused.

In 2000, I went to the rural area in Shannan for fieldwork, and found hundreds of black-neck cranes

Professor Xu Fengxiang (second from right) of Nanjing Forestry College, now known as Nanjing Forestry University, voluntarily went to work in Tibet in the 1980s. She set up the Tibet Plateau Ecological Research Institute in Nyingchi Prefecture, discovered some rare forests with high wood storage and huge trees and wrote a great deal of articles on Tibetan ecological environment.

looking for food in the wilderness. It is rarely known for the black-neck crane--subject to State first-class protection--to gather in large groups. With my camera, I ventured to get closer to them. A country boy followed me. Having examined my camera, he told me: "It is Okay for you to take pictures of them. But you should try not to scare them and throw stones at them. This is village stipulation." Later on, I was told the village rule has been followed for years.

Since the advent of the 1990s, Tibet promulgated more than 20 sets of rules and regulations, including the Regulations of the Tibet Autonomous Region Concerning Environmental Protection. Rules and regulations are being worked out for the protection of nature reserves, wild animals, wild plants, and urban environment.

Technicians from Tibet Water Conservancy Bureau are surveying the water resources of Lhasa River.

A great variety of household appliances in the department store of Lhasa.

Between Tradition and Modernization

Musical Dance Qomolangma

Two events created a hit in Beijing in 1999. They were the "Tibet Cultural Exhibition" early in the year, and the performance of the musical dance Qomolangma in the summer--held to celebrate the 40th anniversary of the Democratic Reform in Tibet.

When the exhibition was held in the Beijing Exhibition Center, the entrance ticket cost 20 yuan, but, despite of the high price, the queue awaiting admission extended for about 1,000 meters.

When the musical dance was performed in the Workers' Gymnasium, all 10,000 seats were filled for each performance. The local people were astonished to see a robust and graceful dance performance emanating from what they understood to be "a cold area with scarce oxygen."

We, who have worked in Tibet, also take pride in the integration of tradition and modernization, which found expression in the musical dance

Traditional folk song and dance performance in Tibet.

performance. Unlike palace dance and monastic dance performance, the modern musical dance performance features traditional dance movements treated in a modern way. As the dance contains modern elements, some in the West cry that cultural tradition has been wiped out in the Tibet. However, the Tibetans do not think that way.

"The world is experiencing rapid development. How can we still live in a traditional village isolated from the outside world?" they ask.

"Why we should not seek changes, whilst the United States and Europe are developing by leaps and bounds?"

"Does this mean changes and development constitute a Western patent?"

Historical Pursuit for Development

Tibet has ventured to carry out two reforms.

The first took place in the early 1900s. Border troubles haunting southwest China convinced the Qing rulers that Tibet was highly likely to be annexed by the British if no remedial measures were taken. Zhang Yingtang was therefore sent to Tibet. He produced a series of rules and regulations for Tibet's administration, which won the endorsement of the Qing Government. The reform began first in the field of Tibet's political system. New organs were set up to strengthen the Central Government's rule over Tibet. Gradually, the reform spread to the agricultural, industrial and business fields, with mineral ores mined, roads built, modern education organized, newspapers launched, and banks set up. The purpose was to build up Tibet economically. Zhang was later replaced by High Commissioner Lian Yu to pursue this goal. However, both failed to win true success.

The second reform took place in the 1920s. During years of exile outside Tibet, the 13th Dalai Lama saw the outside world, and came to understand Tibet was isolated and poverty-stricken. He introduced some reform measures geared to end the discouraging situation. But he failed.

Both reforms failed for the same reasons: They threatened feudal serfdom and the existing system of mixed temporal and religious administration, and damaged the interests of monasteries and serf owners. The British imperialists worked hard to make Tibet a "buffer zone" in their power politics, and further to make Tibet a dependency. For this purpose, they tried hard to ensure Tibet remained as poor as ever. Reform was therefore not allowed in Tibet. This points up the fact that imperialist aggressive forces and feudal serfdom were the largest barriers to social modernization.

Tibetan woman is riding a motorcycle.

Window-shopping.

Liquefied petroleum gas (LPG) has changed Tibetans' life, who used to burn cow dung to cook.

Tibet won peaceful liberation in 1951. Under the leadership of the CPC, the Tibetans drove imperialist forces out of the region, a boon for undertaking the modernization drive. In 1959, the Democratic Reform began; a million Tibetan serfs and slaves won emancipation. The Democratic Reform made it possible for Tibet to follow a political system the same as that in other parts of China. People of various ethnic groups living in China help each other for common development. Alongside with changes in the social, economic and political fields, there is a change in ideological field in Tibet.

Proposal for the "Three-Rivers Project"

All Tibetans know about the "Three-Rivers Project." It refers to the agricultural development in the valleys drained by the middle reaches of the Yarlung Zangbo, Nyang Qu and Lhasa rivers. It covers Nyingchi in the east, Ngari in the west, China's western frontier, and Nagqu in the north, including 18 cities and counties,

231 townships, and 1,890 villages, with a total population of 798,600, or 36.37 percent of the population in Tibet. As the project area is the granary of Tibet, it is of vital importance to the region.

The "Three-River Project" began in 1989, when a contingent of 40 people--including 15 scholars in farming, forestry, animal husbandry, economics and computer science--went to the project area to undertake a six-month survey. On this basis, they worked out a blueprint for development in the area for the following 10 years. Projects covered commodity grain production bases, livestock breeding farms, vegetable farms, light and textile industrial enterprises.

The project lasted from 1991 to 2000, and included some 220 projects. Major ones include:

—Water works: Building 36 irrigation canals totaling 811 km in length, 12 reservoirs with a combined holding capacity of 460 million cubic meters, six pump stations, four flood diversion projects, and three drinking water projects. They are expected to irrigate 70,000 hectares of farmland and 24,000 hectares of trees and grass.

—Crop cultivation: Transforming 82,000 hectares of medium and low-yield farmland, reclaiming 6,700 hectares of farmland, and building some 30,000 hectares of high-yield farmland. The purpose is to set up 10 commodity grain and oil-bearing crops production bases, and 180 hectares of vegetable growing centers in Shannan, Xigaze and Lhasa.

—Animal husbandry: Planting 15,600 hectares of grass, reforming 60,000 hectares of grassland, setting

Students of Xigaze No.2 Middle School are having an English lesson.

up 180 hectares of grass seeds farm, setting up five yak production farms, seven buffalo farms, four pig and chicken farms.

—Forestry: planting 62,000 hectares of forests, setting up three tree seedling farms at the prefectural and city level, and with a total area of 243 hectares, building four shelter tree belts on the banks of the Yarlung Zangbo River, Nyang Qu River and Lhasa River.

—Energy: Building five county-level hydraulic power stations with an installed generating capacity of 10,400 KW, and five power substations; and popularizing the use of 50,000 solar energy stoves.

—Highway construction: Building the Zetang and Donggar Bridge across the Yarlung Zangbo River, and 1,000 km of rural roads.

—Science and technology: Building 14 experimental and exemplary zones, applying 28 technological items to production, expanding and renovating 21 county agro-technological stations, 22 vet and grass supply stations and 20 forestry work stations, and training 500,000 people technologically.

Water diversion project along the Yarlung Zangbo River.

Construction of Reservoirs: Life Project

When we drove through the "three-river" area in 2000, we saw gratifying changes. We left from Zetang, passed by the Tombs of Tubo Kings, and reached Qoingo Township in Qoingyi County. A 47-meter-high dam blocked our vision--the Qoingo Reservoir, the largest water works of the project. Construction of the reservoir began in the summer of 1994, and was commissioned in 1997.

The dam is composed of the work bridge, which is 420 meters long, 47 meters high and 90 meters long, and the flood diversion canal, 233 meters long. The reservoir, with a holding capacity of 11.58 meters, is large enough to irrigate 4,300 hectares of farmland for 20 villages of seven townships, inhabited by 20,000 people. With the per-hectare yield rising from 2,250 kg to 5,250 kg as a result of the reservoir, the county has solved its grain shortage problem.

With water flowing down the area, the 180 hectares of low-yield field were transformed, 260 hectares of slopes were planted with grass, and 530 hectares with trees. Apple, pear, peach and apricot orchards emerged.

Kagar Village in Xietongmoin, Xigaze, has a population of 800. In Tibetan, Kagar means "yellow people", so called mainly because their teeth and bones are yellowed by prolonged drinking of water containing fluorine. After the Democratic Reform, the Central Government dispatched specialists there to treat the sick. However, the problem remained unsolved for a long period of time.

Computer room of hydrological station of Tibet Autonomous Region.

Agricultural technicians of Tibet are estimating the production condition of the experimental field of high-yielding highland barley in Doilungdeqen County.

It was under this situation that a drinking water project was launched in the village area in 1992. A deep well was sunk, a water tower built and a 2.5 km pipe laid to carry healthy drinking water from the county seat to the village. The Central Government invested 920,000 yuan in the project, and the local people call it a "life project". How does the project bear on daily life? Only the residents of Kagar Village can tell clearly.

Altogether, eight reservoirs were built, and there is a moving story behind the construction of each one.

Forest Belts in Shannan Prefecture

Shannan has done a better job of planting trees. We went there on a May day. As my car sped along the forest belt, which is 0.7 km wide and 150 km long and covers some 6,000 hectares, the green environment was deeply impressive.

In the depth of the tree belt were mostly poplar trees

including Beijing poplar, Xinjiang poplar, and six introduced species. They had grown up after six years. Flanking the highway are willow trees, including red willows and weeping willows. We were told there was one kind of willow called "head chopping willow". The locals chop its top branches as firewood, but fresh branches will grow in the following year. It is these short, thick willows that provide firewood for the locals.

The Shannan Tree Seedling Garden covers 56 hectares, with 28 hectares devoted to tree seedlings. Major tree species in the garden include cypress. Our guide told us all the trees planted in the 150-km forest belt came from the garden, which exported 300,000 tree seedlings to Xigaze Prefecture in 1997.

In Gonggar County, home to Gonggar Airport, we were told that sands ate up 200 km of land on the yearly basis, and sandstorms lasted for months, often forcing the airport to suspend operation.

Before the Democratic Reform in 1959, only one tree survived in Gyidexiu Town, Gonggar County. In

Computer controlling room of a small hydro-power station in Gyangze County.

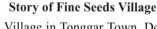
Protective forest belt along the Yarlung Zangbo River.

118

the following 30 years, trees planted in the area all died out. During the "Three-River Project" in 1991, special efforts were made to plant trees, and this time the efforts were crowned with success!

The "Three-River Project" was rounded off in 2001. In 1999, Tibet's grain production reached 917,000 tons, an increase of 7.9 percent from the previous year and 30-fold more than in 1959, when the Democratic Reform was conducted.

Story of Fine Seeds Village

Sangmo Village in Tonggar Town, Doilungdeqen County is famous for its fine varieties of seeds. Over the years, the village introduced 11 fine varieties of seeds from the United States and France. These seeds are adopted in the village before they are sold to other villages. According to the locals, ordinary *qingke* bar-

Yarlung River valley in Shannan Prefecture.

ley sells for 1.6 yuan per kg, and ordinary winter wheat 1.2 yuan per kg. However, fine-variety *qingke* barley sells for 2.6 yuan per kg, and fine-variety winter wheat 2.5 yuan per kg. Fine variety of seeds give high yields. For instance, barley production rises from 2,000 kg to 6,000 kg per hectare, and spring wheat from 3,750 kg to 6,750 kg. In Xigaze, the winter wheat production rises to 12,750 kg per hectare when five varieties of seeds are adopted. It was reported that Tibet has introduced some 80 varieties of fine wheat, *qingke* and rapeseed. Given this situation, many have adopted fine varieties. In 2000, Sangmo Village sold 45,000 kg of fine varieties of seeds at a price of 1.2 yuan per kg more than ordinary seeds.

Scattered farming has its drawbacks as individuals can hardly fight drought and pests. Realizing this, many farmers in Lhasa, Xigaze and Shannan have joined

Agricultural technicians of Tibet are watching the growth of highland barley in the experimental field.

hands voluntarily for mechanized plowing, sowing and harvesting.

The above change is coupled by another change in the importance attached to the market. To cope with market needs, the suburban areas in Lhasa and Xigaze organized to grow vegetables and provide transport services. Some farmers have set up restaurants in cities and stores offering handicrafts, which are loved by tourists. Some villages become specialized in certain fields such as Tibetan knives, cushions, aprons, pottery and traditional writing paper.

It is also fashionable to grow melons and vegetables, and raise domestic animals in the suburban areas of cities and towns. With aid from Shanghai, Gyangze set up a feed additive plant with an annual capacity of 1,500 tons in 2000. Such feed shortens the growing period, a boon for increased meat output. During the slack seasons, the farmers plunge into transport business.

Growing vegetables is lucrative. Recent years saw

Highland barley harvest is expected in Lhunzhub County.

increased consumption of vegetables in cities and towns. To cope with the growing need, households specialized in vegetable growing have emerged in the rural areas of Lhasa, Xigaze and Shannan. Farmers from China's hinterland were also invited to guide the vegetable growing or contract to grow vegetables.

Many locals were astonished to see green vegetables, round watermelons, red tomatoes and long cucumbers in the fields, which used to be covered with wild grass. Modern farming is enriching the market supply and changing the mind of the locals.

"I don't know what modernization is," said an old man. "But, I know how much more grain we harvest today, and how good the farm machinery is."

Vegetable base in Shiquanhe, capital of Ngari Prefecture, has for the first time cultivated huge cucumber.

Telephone Village in Nyingchi

An 80-year-old man named Qunsang Raodain made a phone call to his far-off friend from his own home in Gongzong Village, Bayi Town, Nyingchi Prefecture. Examining the phone set in his wrinkled hand, he could not explain how he could communicate with his absent friend. "Good! It's really good!" he exclaimed.

Cering Norbu's house is as luxurious as those in cities and towns. During our visit to the farmer, he revealed the keys to riches: "With a phone installed at home, I am in a position to develop a transport business."

According to village chief Nyima, the village has some 60 households, and 30 of them have installed telephones. Income from motorized transport business adds up to 3 million yuan a year.

A village accessible to telephones.

122

A satellite TV receiver is installed in the Danggula maintenance squad of Qinghai-Tibet Highway, which enables nearby residents to watch TV.

TV was strange to ordinary Tibetans in the late 1970s. When the first TV set made way into a Tibetan family later, his neighbors swarmed into his courtyard to watch the programs. Statistics show that every 100 households in cities and towns and farmer and herder households in the rural areas own 88 color TV sets and six black-white TV sets. All townships have TV relay stations. People in Lhasa, Xigaze, Zetang, Bayi, Shiquanhe, Nagqu and other major cities and towns have access to 30 TV programs, many of them dubbed in the Tibetan language.

TV programs are not only entertaining but also educational, providing the audience also with information. Purbo Zholma living by Barkor Street places a TV set in front of the Buddhist shrine. "I love *The Panchen Erdeni's Eastward Trip*," she said. "My son loves News and Across the World."

Farmers in Donggar Town, Doilungdeqen, used to complain about too many advertisements in the programs. But, nowadays, they yearn for advertisements, which they think contain information that meets their daily needs. Based on information acquired from TV advertisements, the town has set up cement works, furniture factories and vacation villages with investors from China's hinterland. This prompts many farmers in the town to purchase TV.

If the airplane and telephone have shortened Tibet's distance with the outside world, TV brings the "world" into Tibet. A survey shows that more than 80 percent of the residents of the Barkor Neighborhood Committee in Lhasa watch TV news every day.

A girl in Sog County of northern Tibet is taking a photo in the rapeseed field.

Tibet on Its Own Way to Modernization

It is well known, earth-shattering changes have taken place in Tibet. The problem is that there are still people in the world who wag their fingers at these changes. They bolster their accusation by saying: "It is not strange to see co-existence between traditional and modern things. Tradition will prove too fragile if it is engulfed by modernization. This is not true with regard to the situation in Tibet, where both maintain a respectful distance. Co-existence between traditional and modern things is temporary. They represent two worlds, which are totally unrelated. Their distance will widen with the elapse of time. Modernization is inevitable, and the co-existence between traditional and modern things will be temporary. Given the situation in Tibet, outside force will not be able to pull Tibet into a modern society."

I am not going to make an analysis of the assertion. The fact is that the Tibetans think development is the only way out for them to live a better life. They don't worry about losing traditional things because of development.

Holy Eagle is a song written by Zhaxi Dawa, a friend of mine. It reads in part:

At the place where the sun rises every day,
The silver holy eagle comes to the ancient land.
People hailing from outside the snowy land,
They are stewardesses beautiful as fairy maids.
Roads, which our ancestors failed to take,
Oh, holy eagle,
Changes the land at the wink of eyes.

The grand U-turn of the Yarlung Zangbo River.

Imposing scene of Tarmo on the southeast slope of Mount Qomolangma.

Nangbokangri Peak in the west end of Himalayas.

Oh, misty mountains,

Oh, distant roads,

Who flies between heaven and earth?

Ah, it is you, the holy eagle, who takes my wishes far and wide.

My heart goes with the holy eagle, to the distant sky,

For a bird's eye view of the lit-up city and blue sky.

When my dream comes true and I walk into the plane cabin,

And look down on the world with hot tears in eyes,

Footsteps of forefathers on pilgrimage mission still resound.

Ah, holy eagle,

I have parted yesterday and found the light of life.

Oh, gentle wind,

Oh, gentle breeze,

Son of the blue sky returns to the hometown.

Ah, holy eagle, you make my childhood dream become true.

I didn't pay much attention to the song as it eulogizes the aircraft, a modern transport vehicle. Facts prove I was wrong. The Tibetans sang it in the past and even at present. Wherever we went during our trip, we heard people singing the song. It shows the Tibetans' love for modern things. Like people in modern world yearn for wind and snow in the snow-bound land, people in Tibet yearn for city lamps and the light of modern lives.

Actually, the song sings the praises of Zhaxi Cering, the first-generation pilot of the Tibetan ethnic group. A friend of mine interviewed him once, and was told

Gonggar International Airport of Lhasa is available for Boeing 747 and Airbus A340 to take off and land. At present, the Lhasa airport has mainly Airbus A340 and Boeing 757 aircrafts.

he was born in 1954 into a poor peasant family in Garze County. He has six elder brothers and two elder sisters. To eke out a living, his parents worked with might and main in the field. All of his elder brothers died of hunger and illness before the peaceful liberation of Tibet in 1951. When Zhaxi was born, his parents prayed to the Buddha he would survive. A Living Buddha was invited to name the boy Zhaxi Cering meaning "auspiciousness and long life."

Talking about his pilot career, however, Zhaxi Cering said, "I can be a pilot not because of the name. I live in a good period of time."

Zhaxi has become an auspicious bird in the eyes of the Tibetans. The song expresses their wish for a better world. It is therefore inhuman for the West to wish to turn the traditional culture of Tibet into a living fossil.

My conclusion is that Tibet is moving its own way between traditional and modern things. Tibet will have a brighter future.

The festive Potala Palace.